COMFORT CLOTHES

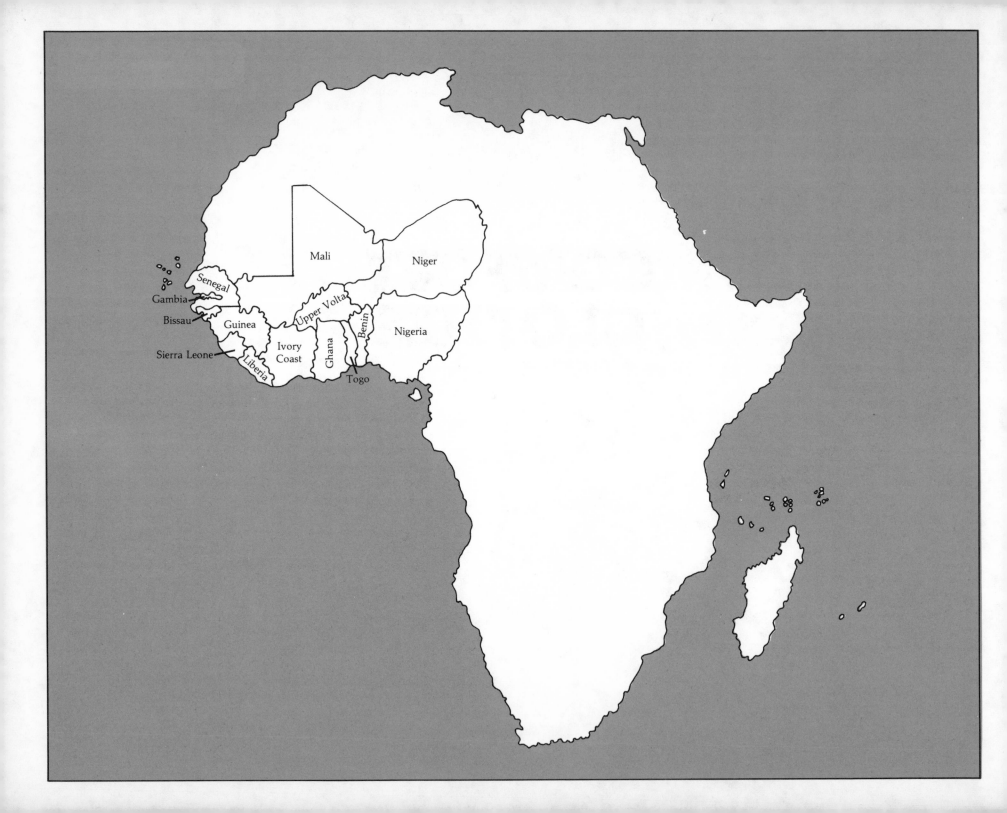

COMFORT CLOTHES

Easy to Make and Easy to Wear
West African Garments

Chris Rex

Illustrations by Lee Fitzgerrell

Celestial Arts
Millbrae, California

I dedicate this book to
my mom,
my dad,
and, my husband, Ben
who have unfailingly supported my efforts

Celestial Arts
231 Adrian Rd.
Millbrae, CA 94030

First Printing, May 1981

Manufactured in the United States of America

Library of Congress Cataloging in Publication Data

Rex, Christine, 1945–
  Comfort clothes.

  1. Clothing and dress.   2. Costume—Africa, West.
I. Title.
TT560.R49   646.4'3   80-69534
ISBN 0-89087-321-7 (pbk.)

1 2 3 4 5 6 7   87 86 85 84 83 82 81

TABLE OF CONTENTS

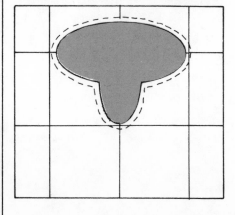

ACKNOWLEDGMENTS

So many people were important in helping this book come together. My thanks to Terry Stanley for planting the seed, to Laura Lamar for her fine design work on the mock-up, to American River College for enabling me to take my sabbatical leave for research in West Africa in 1975, to Edna Chandler, Dick and Beany Wezelman and Esther Dendel who all helped prepare me for my field work. Thanks also to my African friends, Micaidou Dia, Amy Olaopa, Judith and Akilagpa Sawyerr and Dorothy Cooper who helped me along the way, to Renee Boser for her help and encouragement, to Inge Helm for her translation, to Bompossa N'Silk who shared her methods, Bill Welmers who helped with African words, Bob Mansergh for his critical help with my manuscript. Thanks to my proofreaders: Heather Mansergh, Colleen Miner, Colleen Malone, and my mother, Ruth E. Rex. And finally my thanks to my illustrator, Lee Fitzgerrell, who translated from my thoughts and photos into these fine illustrations.

INTRODUCTION

Since the turn of this century the western world has appreciated the art of West Africa, especially its sculpture. However, little has been written about the fantastic textile arts and even less about the regal clothing worn now in daily life. I have written this book because of my desire to share with you my fascination with the clothing of this part of the world and my interest in its people.

While this clothing draws on a rich African heritage, it often shows influences of Arab and western fashion, from both colonial times and present-day. The patterns presented are all representative of those worn daily in most contemporary West African countries. The people in these societies value quality cloth and clothing highly. They cherish traditional approaches while, at the same time encouraging new creative design.

This book is set up in chapters of related garments. At the back of the book you will find a Measurement Chart to guide you in making adjustments to the patterns for your own figure. Also, you will find a series of full-size Neck Opening Templates. Many of these outfits are appropriate for children's wear; simply use their small measurements in place of yours.

This gathering of clothing and methods of decorations is in no way complete. African clothing and cloth has abundant variety. Many regions have distinct styles. The outfits shown here do represent styles seen in many parts of West Africa today and the fabric decoration includes the major techniques.

GENERAL SEWING INFORMATION

Although I assume a basic understanding of sewing, none of the outfits use complex construction. The flattering draped nature of most West African garments lends itself to easy fitting and the use of a wide variety of fabrics.

Always preshrink your fabric before cutting.

In most cases, you will want to make a paper pattern before marking and cutting your fabric. As diagrammed, all patterns fit a size 12. Be sure to adjust to your personal measurements as suggested for each garment. When marking your cloth, fabric marker which can be wiped off with water (such as the Wonder Marker by Collins Inc.) is the simplest method. All patterns are figured with ½" seam allowance.

You can easily interchange the various neck openings shown in the Neck Opening Templates. Each template is full size. Half the neck is given, so you will want to trace the shape on folded paper, cut, then unfold for your complete neck opening pattern. Measure around your head at the widest place (usually at the nose) and compare that with the template to be sure of a good fit. Most neck openings will hold their shape best if a pellon interfacing is cut and sewn as one piece with the neck facing.

Few of these garments have darts, since they tend not to be fitted. However, where darts do occur on skirts or pants they are 2" wide and 6" long. Bust darts from the side seams are 2" wide. The length should be determined by your personal bust measurement. To get the best fit over your bust, measure from the shoulder down to the tip of the bust. Also measure the bust span (see Measurement Chart). Mark these measurements on your paper pattern. The dart should never go beyond the bust tip. It gives the best fit when it comes to approximately 1" from the tip. Bust darts from the waist-band are 1" wide. Their length is related to the bust measurement suggested above. These darts should come approximately 1" below the bust tip.

On full-length garments a shoulder-to-floor measurement is suggested. This allows for a 2" hem. Your hem line is then 2" off the floor. If you prefer either a higher or lower hem, allow for this difference in fabric length as you cut.

When sewing curves, such as underarms and around neck openings, it is important to remove the extra bulk of the seam. After sewing, trim the curve to a ¼" seam. Then clip as indicated, to the line of stitching, but not through it. An outside curve (A) should be snipped; these slits will spread naturally. An inside curve (B) should be notched, taking out small V shaped snips of excess fabric at intervals of approximately 1".

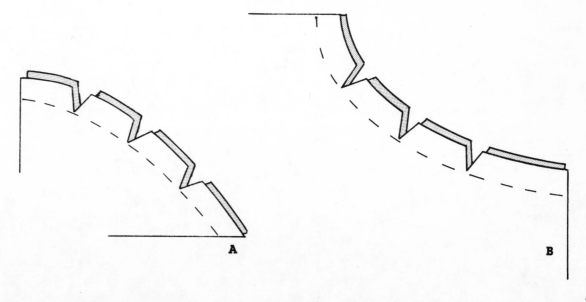

A   B

CHAPTER 1/CAFTANS

BELTED CAFTAN

West African women have adapted the long robe worn by the men (see chapter 4, Riga) to create a caftan with a belted front and free hanging back. This caftan is constructed by joining three long panels.

Fabric Needed:

Measure from your shoulder ridge to the floor, adjusting for desired length plus 2" hem allowance (see appendix, Measurement Chart). Multiply this figure by two to get the length of fabric required for the three panels. The three main panels are each 15" wide, so you can cut all three panels from 45" width fabric. Add 12" more for neck facing and belt.

Total fabric suggested for average height (5'6"): 3½ yards of 45" fabric, thread, 1" wide elastic, and hook (see illustration).

Cutting and Construction:

1 Mark shoulder line (shoulder ridge to hem measurement) on the cloth with fabric marker. Mark the 45" width fabric at 15" and 30" intervals and cut the three panels (A). Next, choose your neck opening (see appendix, Neck Opening Templates) and mark it on the center panel of the caftan and on a separate piece of fabric for the neck facing (B). Template VI is shown on the illustration. Be sure to line up the shoulder line on the template with the shoulder line marked on the panel. Then, mark fabric for curved belt (C).

To determine where to belt the caftan for your figure, measure from your shoulder ridge over your bust, to either your natural waist or, if a high waist (Empire look) is desired, measure to that point under the bust. Add ½" seam allowance. This will be the measurement of your bodice in the center panel. Cut all pieces.

2 Turn under ½" on outer edge of the neck facing; press and topstitch. Now, sew the neck facing to the center panel, right sides together, lining up the neck openings marked on each piece. Clip and

trim seam curves; turn facing inside and press. Topstitch or tack the facing in place.

3 Make gathers at the lower edge of the bodice by sewing two rows of long basting stitches and easing the piece to fit the top curve of the belt. Pin upper curve of belt to gathered bodice edge, right sides together; stitch and press flat. Make pleats as indicated on lower center panel by overlapping inner pleat mark to meet outer pleat mark on each side; pin and baste in place. Sew this pleated edge, right sides together, to the bottom curve of the belt. Press seam flat. Your center panel is now complete.

4 Sew the caftan side panels to the center panel, right sides together. Press seams open. Fold the caftan, right sides together, so that the front and back hems meet. To allow for armholes, mark 12" down from the shoulder on the outer edge. Pin front to back along sides and sew each side closed to arm opening. Press side seams open. Turn under, press and topstitch a ½" edge around the arm openings. Hem caftan.

5 On the inside of the dress, sew a tie or wide elastic (1") band to each end of side seam of center belt. Wrap these comfortably around your ribs and fasten with a 1" hook and loop (D). This fits the front and allows the back to flow freely.

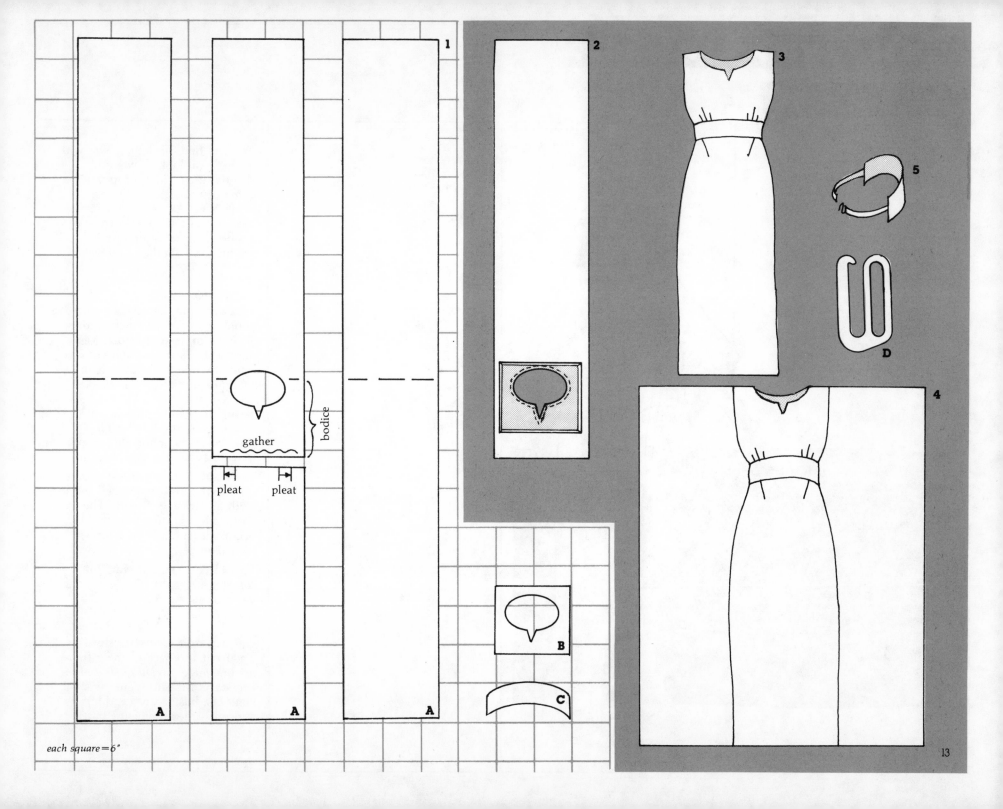

each square=6"

13

POINTED-SLEEVE CAFTAN

You will find this long gown, with its medieval-look sleeves and slightly fitted cut, appropriate for either casual or formal wear. While West African women have been influenced by western clothing, strong tradition predominates in their garment design.

Fabric Needed:
Measure from the ridge of your shoulder to desired length adding 2″ for hem, (see appendix, Measurement Chart). Multiply this figure by two to get the length of fabric required for your Pointed-Sleeve Caftan. Add 12″ for neck facing. In the illustration, an elaborate, decorative facing is reversed to hang outside and provide an additional design feature.

The width of this garment is based on the width of commercial cotton cloth in Africa, 36″ wide. The pattern lends itself to a border print or a print with a large central medallion design.

Total fabric suggested for average height (5'6"): 3⅔ yards of 36″, or 3¼ yards of 45″ cloth, thread.

Cutting and Construction:
The front and back of the caftan are one piece; *no shoulder seam is necessary.* Measure your personal contours: bust, waist, and hips (see appendix, Measurement Chart).

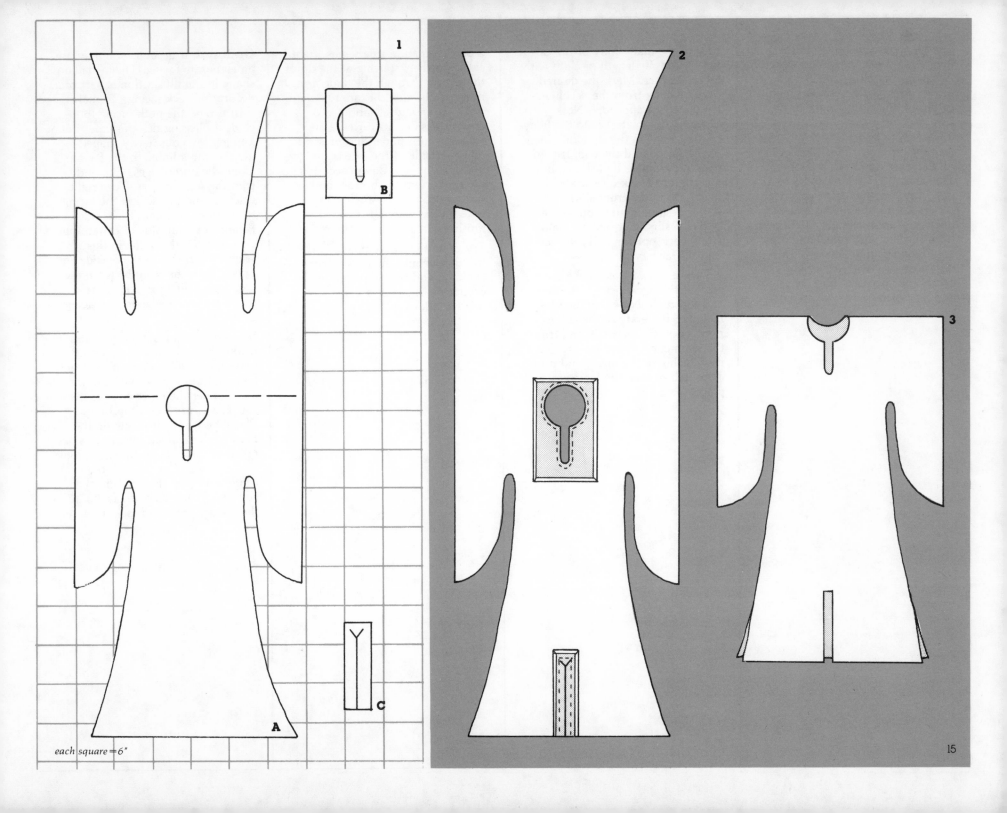

each square = 6"

1

B

C

A

2

3

15

The measurements given in the diagram are for an average size 12. Adjust for larger or smaller proportions. As you draw your caftan on the cloth, check to be sure that the measurement from underarm to underarm is ½ your bust measurement plus 2½″ both on the front and back sections. This allows ½″ seams and a total of 4″ for ease in putting on your caftan. Check the measurements for waist (approximately 16″ down from the shoulder ridge) and hips (approximately 20″ down). These distances vary with each figure; check your personal bust, waist and hip levels.

1 Mark the main body of the caftan (A) on the length of cloth with fabric marker. Mark the desired neck opening from the neckline template (see appendix, Neck Opening Templates) onto the body of the caftan so the shoulder lines of the caftan and the template match. Template II is shown in the illustration. Mark a separate neck facing (B) and a front slit facing (C), if desired in addition to the two side slits. Cut out the main front/back portion and the neck and slit facings.

2 Turn under ½″ along the outer edge of the neck facing (B), press and topstitch. Now sew the neck facing to the body of the caftan, right sides together; clip and trim the seam curves after sewing. Turn neck facing to the inside and press. Topstitch or tack the facing in place.

3 Sew the caftan side seams, right sides together, starting at the tip of the sleeve, through the underarm, down to the side slit (approximately 17″ from end of fabric). To create the side slits for ease in walking, turn under and press ½″ on either side of the side seam opening and sew down, securing the edge. Hem the bottom and turn under and topstitch a ½″ edge on the sleeves for a nice finish.

Try tying the sleeve points together behind the neck while cooking, and untying them while entertaining guests; a very attractive variation.

Optional: If desired, you may use an elaborate facing. The medallion shape in the illustration is part of a decorative neck facing. To make this, extend the neck facing to include a pleasing design shape. Cut a lining for your newly shaped facing. Sew this lining to the facing along the outer edges. Clip and trim the seam curves. Turn right side out and press. Sew the facing to the neck opening; Right side of facing to wrong side of caftan (but do not catch the lining in this seam). Turn this to the outside and press. Tuck the seam between the facing and the lining. Hand sew the loose lining edge to the facing at the neck edge.

If you desire a front slit in addition to the two side slits, measure up from the middle point on the front hem and mark a 17″ vertical line. Turn under the outer edge of the slit facing, press and topstitch. Place the front slit facing on the marked vertical slit line, right sides together. Sew the opening 17″ long and 1″ wide. Cut through the center and snip diagonals to the corners. Trim. Turn the facing to the inside; press and tack in place.

CONTOUR CAFTAN

You can quickly and easily construct this very simple garment. Since its dimensions are determined by the individual's measurements there is no problem in making it your size. The lines and fall of the Contour Caftan are flattering on virtually everyone. The simplicity of this pattern lends itself to elaborate embroidery. West African women can be seen strolling through the markets, as well as at festivities, in their elegantly flowing batiked and tie-dyed contour caftans.

Fabric Needed:

This pattern requires a fabric equally attractive on both sides. In Africa, cotton is the most popular cloth because of its ability to breathe. The native woman usually thinks of a dress length as 3 meters (3 yards 10 inches). Adjust for either the extra-tall or the extra-short person. Measure from the ridge of your shoulder (see appendix, Measurement Chart) to the floor, adjusting for desired length plus hem, and multiply by two. This gives you the length needed for the basic body of the caftan from the floor, over the shoulder and back to the floor. The neck facing requires a rectangle 12" by 15", but need not be of the same fabric. If you wish to add the optional sleeves, allow another 12" of yardage for each sleeve.

Most cotton cloth in Africa is sold in the 36" width. Without the added sleeve this gives a draped sleeve effect coming to just above the elbow. If you wish a longer sleeve, add the optional sleeves. If you are working with 45" wide fabric, it will drape just below the elbow without added sleeves.

Total fabric suggested for average height (5'6"): 3⅓ yards of 36" fabric without sleeve; 4 yards of 36" fabric with sleeves; 3⅓ yards of 45" wide fabric without sleeve. Thread.

Cutting and Construction:

1 Mark your shoulder to floor measurement on the cloth with fabric marker. Choose the desired neckline template (see appendix, Neck Opening Templates). Template III is shown in the illustration. Mark it on the body of the caftan and then on a separate piece of fabric for your neck facing. Be sure your shoulder line mark coincides with the shoulder line on the template.

Cut the front and back of the caftan in one piece (A); *no shoulder seam is necessary.* Cut the neck facing (B). Cut the sleeves (C), if desired, and mark the shoulder line on them (exact center). Turn under the outer edge of the neck facing ½", press and topstitch.

2 Sew the neck facing to the body of the caftan, right sides together; clip and trim the seam curves after sewing. Turn facing inside and press. Topstitch or tack the facing in place.

Sew the sleeves (optional) to the body of the caftan, right sides together, being sure to match up the shoulder line marks on both. Press seams open. Turn under the outer edge of the sleeves ½" for a nice finish.

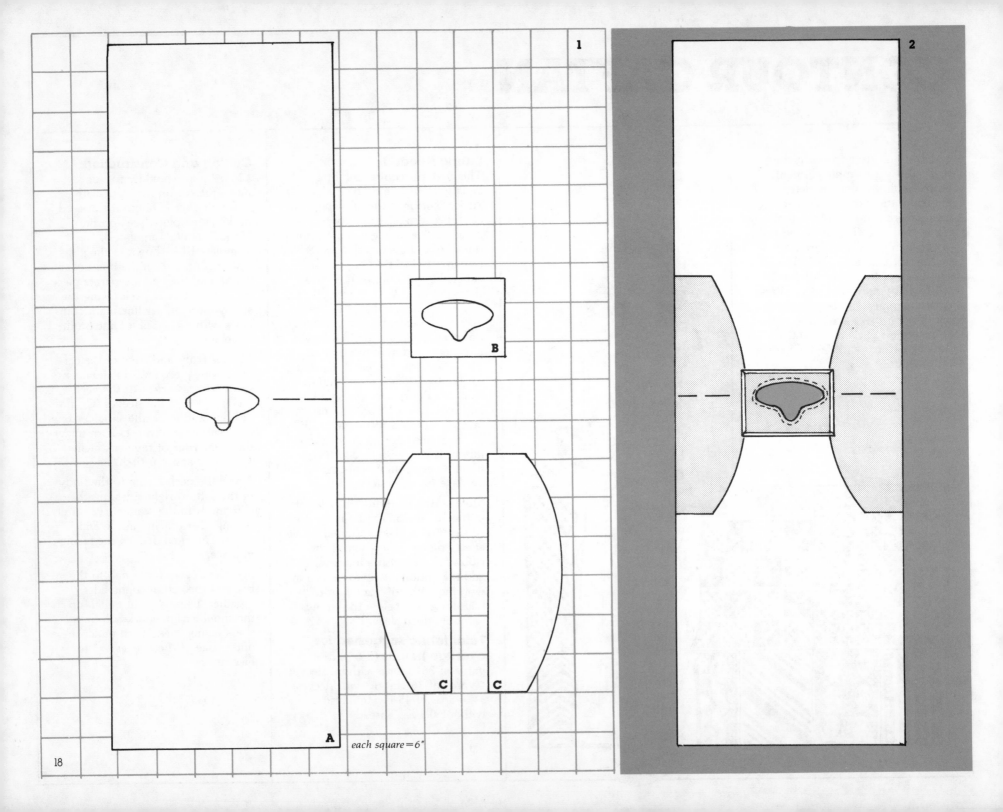

B

A

each square=6"

C   C

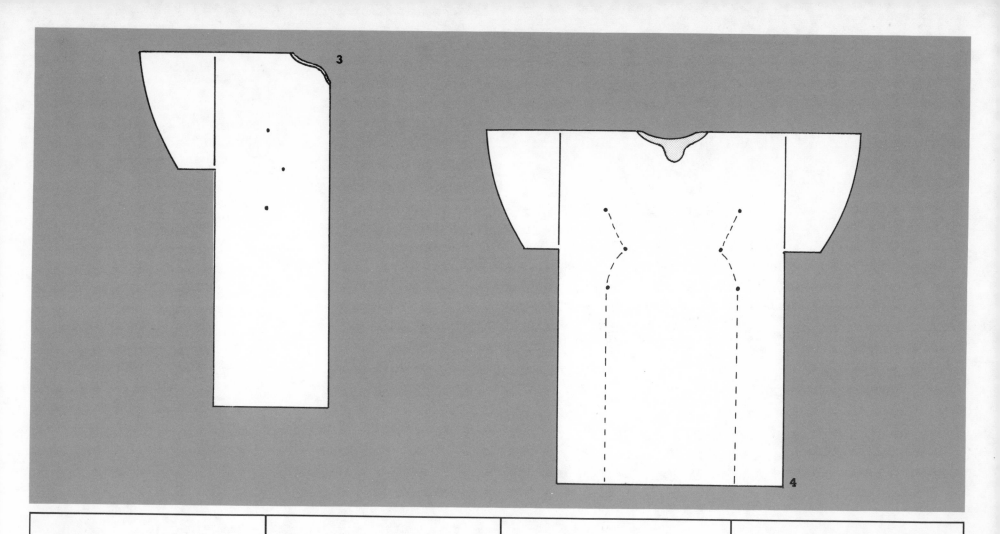

3 Measure your personal contours: bust, waist, and hips. Fold your caftan at the shoulder line so that the front is laying evenly on the back, wrong sides together; pin in place. Now fold this in half lengthwise, thus giving you a center line for accurate mapping of your contours. Always measure your contours from this center line.

On the right quarter, approximately 10" down (use your specific measurement) from your shoulder line start your contour line. From center fold, mark a point ¼ of your bust measurement plus 2" (when multiplied by 4 you have your figure plus 8" of extra looseness for easily putting on the garment). Next, mark a point approximately 16" down from the shoulder which is ¼ of your waist

measurement plus 2". Approximately 20" down from the shoulder line, mark a point from center fold that is ¼ of your hip measurement plus 2". Now with marker, connect these points with a curved line to form your contour. Mark the same points on the left quarter.

4 Now unfold lengthwise and sew back to front, *wrong sides together*, starting from the bust mark, connecting to the waist mark, the hip mark and to the bottom of the caftan. Hem the bottom. The large exterior seam allowance flows elegantly as you walk.

DOUBLE WRAPPED DRESS

CHAPTER 2/
WRAPPED GARMENTS

DOUBLE WRAPPED DRESS

The wraparound is a natural for Africans who have draped themselves in fine cloth for centuries. This dress wraps in two directions for a comfortable and secure fit. How you cut the cloth determines how it will fit and hang on you.

Fabric Needed:

Measure from your shoulder ridge to the floor (see appendix, Measurement Chart). Adjust for desired length and add 2″ for hem. Multiply this figure by two, to get the length of fabric required for the main portion of the Double Wrap Dress. Add 1⅓ yards for sash and neck facing.

Total fabric suggested for average height (5'6"): 4⅓ yards of 45″ wide cloth, thread, velcro or other fasteners.

Cutting and Construction:

1 Mark the main portion of the dress (A) and the side contours of the pattern as indicated. Mark the neck opening. The front and back of the dress are all one piece; *no shoulder seam is necessary.* Mark neck facing (B) and the two long sashes (C). Cut.

2 Turn under ½″ along the outer edge of the neck facing; press and topstitch. Place the neck facing on the main body of the dress, right sides together, lining up the neck openings. Pin and sew. Clip and trim seam. Turn facing to the inside and press. Topstitch or tack the facing in place.

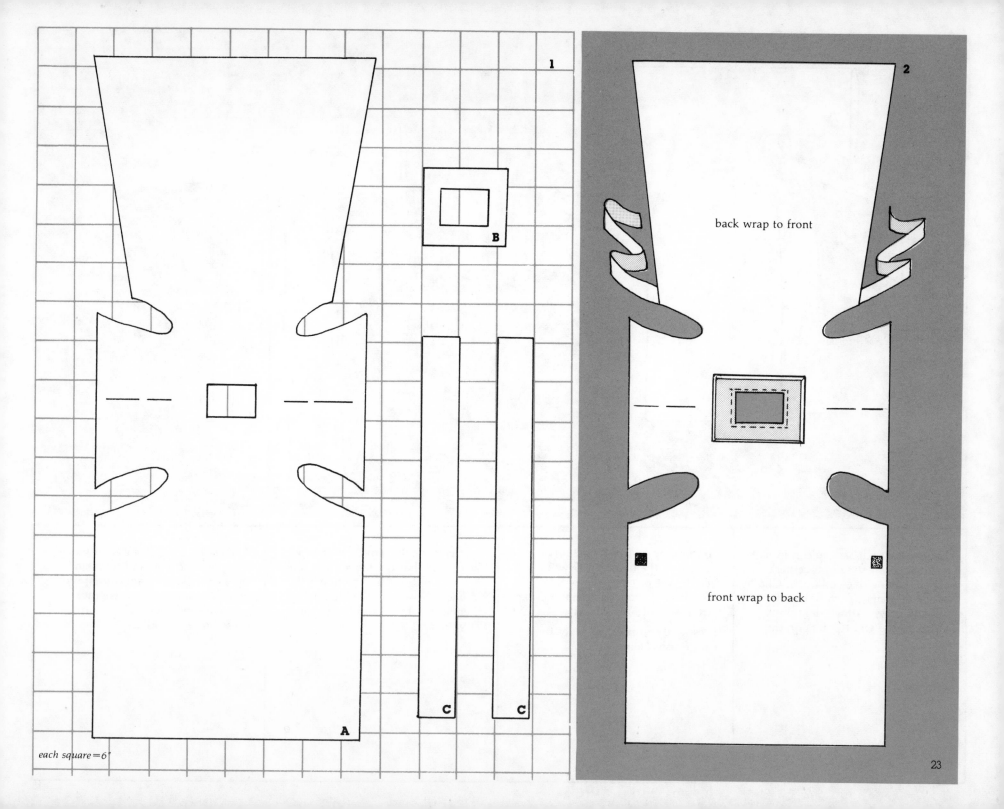

1

B

A

C C

each square = 6"

2

back wrap to front

front wrap to back

23

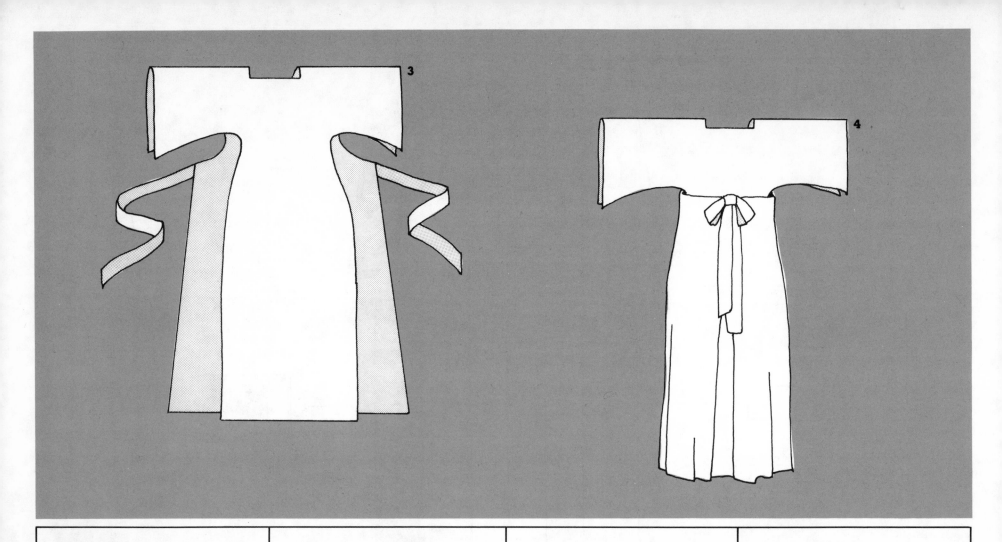

To prepare each sash fold it in half lengthwise, right sides together. Sew it leaving one end open. Clip and trim seams. Turn right side out and press. Attach the two sashes to the waist points on the "back-wrap-to-front" section as indicated in the diagram. Sew 2" velcro tabs or other desired fasteners on the waist points of the "front-wrap-to-back" section.

Press and topstitch all edges for a neat finish. Hem.

3 Lower the neck over your head; be certain that the tab section falls in front and the sash section falls in back. Now take the tabs, wrap them around you and fasten them at your back.

4 Then take the sashes and wrap them around you and tie them in the front. Equally appropriate for a beach cover or hostess gown, you will find the double wrap dress quite versatile.

WRAPPED PANTS AND WRAPPED TOP

Since the earliest appearance of European traders, western fashion has had an impact on African styles. Among the Krio* of Sierra Leone, traditional dress is based on 19th century western fashions. African adaptations, however, usually keep pace with western trends. This outfit of wrapped pants and wrapped top combines contemporary flair with the traditional wrap approach.

Fabric Needed:

To find the amount of fabric needed for the Wrapped Pants, measure your normal pant length and allow 10" for hem and drawstring casing. Multiply this figure by two and add 6" for the drawstring. The top requires approximately 1¼ yards plus 1¼ yards of lining fabric.

Total fabric suggested for average height (5'6"): Wrapped Pants, 2½" yards of 45" fabric. Wrapped Top, 1¼ yards of 45" fabric plus 1¼ yards of lining fabric, thread, 1" wide elastic, interlocking hooks.

Wrapped Top
Cutting and Construction:

1 Check your bust and waist measurements (see appendix, Measurement Chart). Add or subtract on the side seams to fit your figure. The top shown in the diagram is a size 12, but fits several sizes because of its wrapped style. Mark the three pieces (C) with your size adjustments onto the cloth with fabric marker and cut.

2 Sew darts as indicated (see General Sewing Information) and press to the side. Place the two back pieces, right side to right side, on the front and pin the side seams. Sew and press seams open. Proceed with the lining in the same manner. Pin elastic with interlocking hooks on the ends of the back sections of the top fabric. With right sides together, place the lining on the fabric and sew only the following seams: the two ends (with elastic facing *in*), the two back slopes, the two armholes, and the neck opening. Turn the lining right side out and press.

*Krio (KREE-oh)

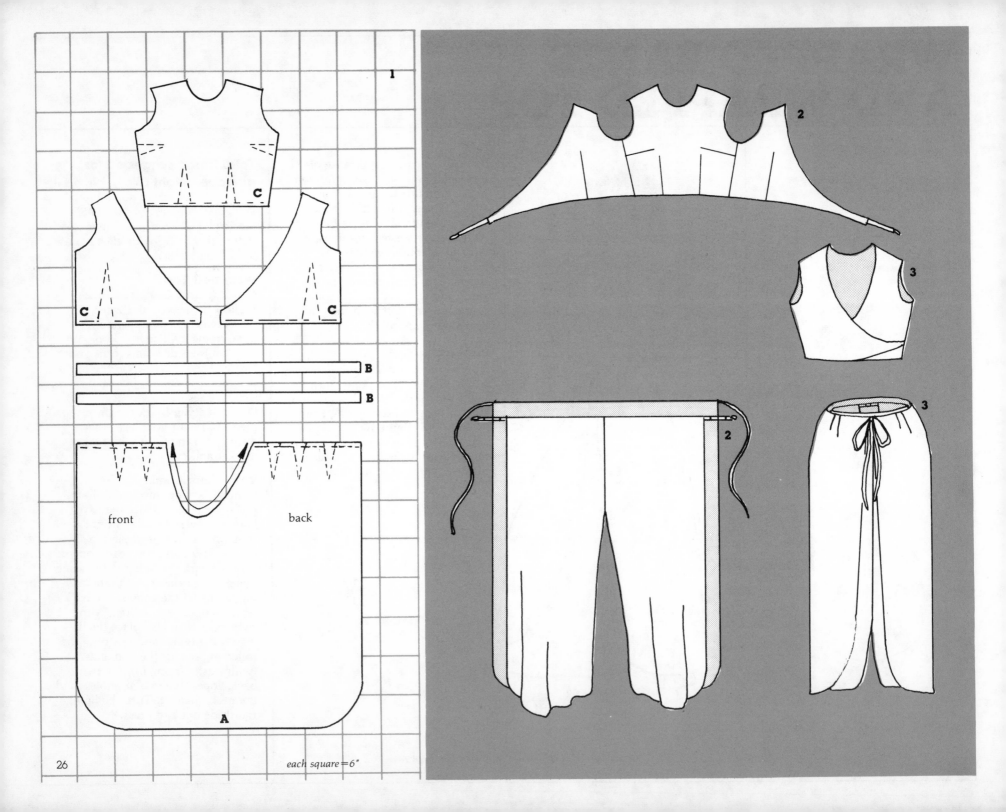

1

C

C

C

B

B

front   back

A

2

3

2

3

26   *each square = 6"*

3 With right sides together sew the shoulder seams of the top fabric. Sew the lining at the shoulder seam by hand. Make a slot in the right side seam approximately 1″ long and 1″ above the finished bottom edge. You can do this by opening the seam of both fabric and lining and topstitching around the opening, joining the two pieces of cloth. Now press and sew the hem. Place the high neck in front. Cross the sloping sections in back. Bring the left section on top and through the side slot. Hook together underneath the garment in front.

Pants
Cutting and Construction:

1 Before marking the pants pattern on your cloth with fabric marker, determine both your pant length and your crotch measurement. To find your crotch measurement, place a measuring tape at your waistline in front, run it between your legs and to your waistline in back. Allow for seams and drawstring casing. The crotch of the pattern (see arrow) should measure 2″ more than your actual measurement for ease of movement. To make it larger, simply move the waistline up. To make it smaller, move the waistline down. Mark and cut two of the pants pattern pieces (A), one with the pattern right side up and one with the pattern right side down. Mark and cut sashes, (B).

2 Sew the darts as indicated and press. Place the two pants pieces together, right side to right side, and sew the crotch seam. Clip and trim the curve and press open. On the back-wrap-to-front section fold the waist under ½″ and press. Fold that pressed edge under 2″, press and sew. This forms the casing for the drawstring. Fold under ½″ on all raw edges and the hem; press and topstitch. Sew the two drawstring sections together to form one long drawstring. Fold in ½″ on all raw edges and press. Now fold lengthwise and topstitch. Thread drawstring through casing. Attach elastic with an interlocking hook onto each end of the waistband on the smaller front-wrap-to-back section.

3 Step into your pants with the elastic connectors in front and the drawstring section in back. First wrap the front around to the back and hook the elastic bands together. Now wrap the back around to the front; gather and distribute any fullness and tie the drawstring in front.

This outfit, with its full pants and bare midriff, has a jaunty appeal and its loose open quality is quite comfortable on hot summer days or elegant in a fancy cloth for evening wear.

WRAPAROUND SKIRT WITH OVAL CAPE TOP

Since early times African women have wrapped themselves in cloth. This outfit is a simple and stream-lined variation on the more bulky traditional approach (see Lappa, Chapter 3). The Oval Cape Top lends an air of elegance. You might easily see this outfit in richly tie-dyed satin at a dinner or special function in one of West Africa's capital cities.

Total fabric suggested for average height (5'6"): 3⅔ yards of 45" wide fabric, thread, 2 large snaps.

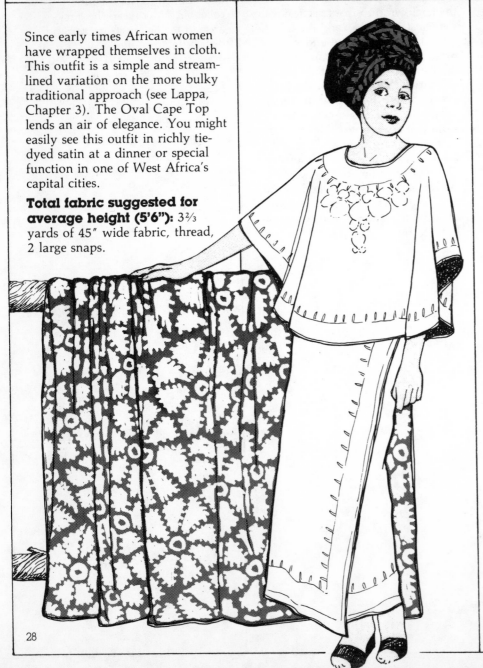

Cutting and Construction:

1 Cut 1¾ yards of 45" width cloth for the skirt (A). Keep in mind that the selvages form the waist and hem. Turn under each raw edge 1" and press, turn that under 2" more, press and topstitch. Cut 1½ yards of 45" wide cloth for the Oval Cape Top (B). Mark the curved front and back of the top.

Now choose your neckline (see appendix, Neck Opening Templates) and place the chosen neck template in the center of the fabric for the top. Template IV is shown in the illustration. Mark, keeping in mind that the selvages are the sides of the cape top. Also mark the neck opening on another piece of cloth to become the neck facing (C).

Figure skirt darts by first determin-ing your waist measurement (diagram is figured for a 26" waist). Each pair of darts sit over each of your hips as you wrap the skirt. This will enable you to have a good fit at the waist and over the hips. Start from the border edge of the skirt and measure ½ your waist plus 2". Mark that point (see crosses in diagram). Go on from there and measure ½ your waist plus 4" and mark. Now make a dart 2½" out on either side of each mark (see crosses). These darts are 6" long and 2" wide at the waist edge. You will have 5 or 6 darts depending on your measurement. Sew darts and

press them away from your marked side points.

Fold over the ties (D) so that all rough edges are inside, press and topstitch. Now attach the ties to either end of the waist. Hem the skirt for your height.

2 Turn under the outer edge of the neck facing ½", press and top-stitch. Place the neck facing on the cape top, right sides together. Pin and sew. Turn the facing to the in-side, press and tack in place or topstitch. Make a 3" hem around the outer edge of the entire cape top. Sew on large snaps, as in-dicated by xs, so that they will each attach front to back. The Africans do not secure the front and back; however, for western modesty the snaps are quite ade-quate to hold the garment in place.

3 To put on your skirt place the darts closest to the inner edge on your right hip and wrap counter-clockwise around the front to the left, around the back to the right and across the front finishing with the border edge front left. The border edge lends itself to a special design. In West African countries it is often embroidered. While em-broidery is now done with treadle sewing machines, it is inspired by the silk hand embroidery of the Hausa* tribe of northern Nigeria (see Chapter 5, Embroidery).

*Hausa (HOW-sah)

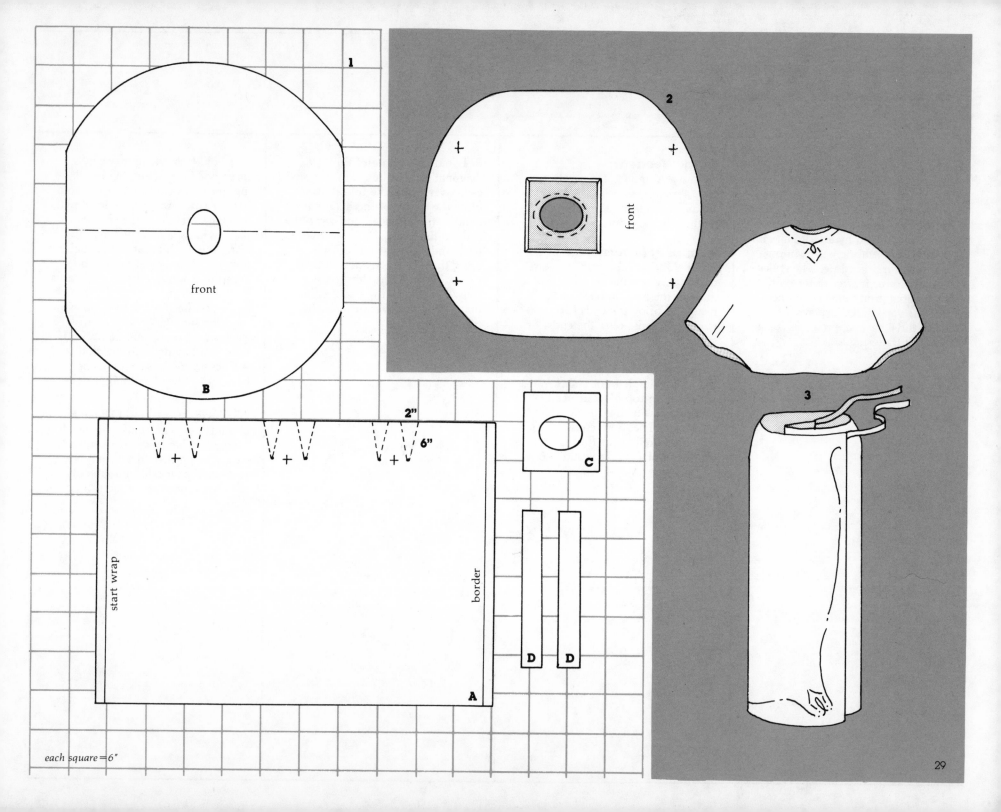

1

front

B

2"

6"

start wrap

border

A

each square = 6"

2

front

C

D D

3

29

HEAD-TIES

The women of West Africa usually wear a head-tie (called a gele* by the Yoruba†) whenever they leave the house. In Mali the style is close to the head with a soft fabric. In Yorubaland (southwestern Nigeria) a stiff, bulky fabric wraps into a tall sculptural head-tie. The styles and choice of fabrics differ with each tribal group and are endless in their variations. Try any of these three basic approaches for a fun and flattering look.

Fabric Needed:
Versions A and C, 1½ yards of 45" fabric; version B, a 45" square. Choose a fabric that is neither slippery nor too bulky.

Wrapping (3 versions):
A. 1 Fold your fabric on the diagonal. Place the center at the nape of the neck in back of the head and bring the ends forward.   **2** Cross over the ends. Be sure they lie flat and don't bunch cord-like as you bring the ends around to the back again and tie them in a simple knot.   **3** Arrange the cloth on top of your head, pulling and tucking to get a pleasing shape. The loose ends can be left, or tucked in, or fluffed and pinned in place to look like a bow.

B. 1 Fold the square of fabric diagonally. Then fold the diagonal edge over. With the fold under, place the center of the diagonal high on the forehead and wrap the ends to the back.   **2** Cross over in back and twist the ends. Then bring them to the front and tie them.   **3** Tuck the third corner (now hanging in the back) either under the crossover or over the crossover.

C. 1 Fold fabric lengthwise in three.   **2** Start wrapping by placing one end of the cloth over your left ear (the end should face down and back). Hold that firmly in place with one hand while you bring the cloth up at a diagonal towards the front of your head. Wrap it around and down towards the back. Bring it around the back and over the starting end.   **3** Now hold the same area firmly (there are now 2 layers) and go around your head again with the cloth.   **4** Tuck in the loose end at the back of the head, folding it over the previous wrap.

While versions A and C have an elegant sculptural look, version B is soft and feminine. African women can wrap their heads in a few seconds, but it will undoubtedly take some practice to learn this skill.

*gele (GEH-leh)

†Yoruba (YOH-roo-bah)

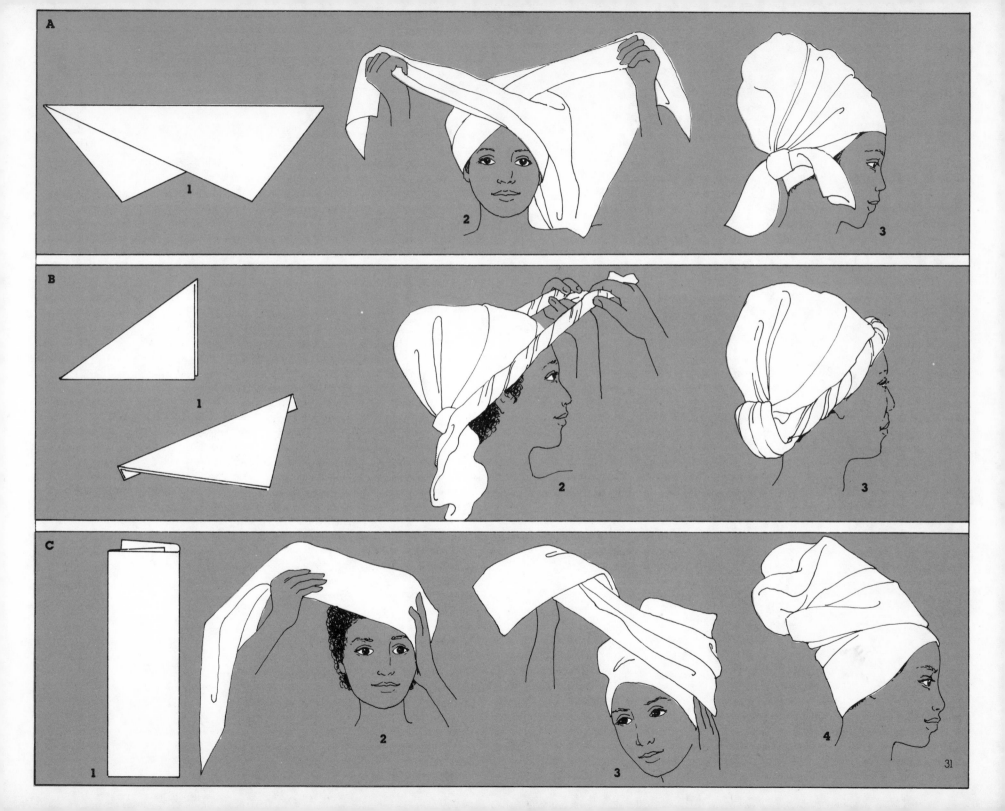

A

1

2

3

B

1

2

3

C

1

2

3

4

31

CHAPTER 3/
REGIONAL GARMENTS

THE LAPPA* AND THE LIBERIAN BLOUSE

Throughout West Africa women wear the lappa, the predominant women's garb for centuries. Some tribal groups call it a "wrapper" and it is just that, a length of cloth wrapped around hips and legs and rolled at the waist.

In many tribes the women choose a loosely fitting blouse to accompany the lappa. However, in Liberia and Sierra Leone they prefer a fitted top such as this raglan sleeved, panel front version.

Total fabric suggested for average build (5'6") Lappa, 1½ yards of 45" cloth; Liberian Blouse, 1½ yards of 45" fabric or 1⅔ yards of a fabric with a definite direction to the design.

The Liberian Blouse Cutting and Construction:

1 Before you mark the fabric, measure your bust, waist and bust span (see appendix, Measurement Chart). The Liberian Blouse is designed to have a fitted look, yet is loose enough to put on over your head. Check that the total measurement at the bust line of the back, front, right and left side panels equals your bust plus 4" total seam allowance *and* 4" of ease. Also check that the width of the bustline of your front panel equals your bust span plus 1" for the total seam allowance on that piece.

Now mark all pieces with any necessary size changes onto your cloth with fabric marker and cut.

2 Sew bust darts as indicated (see General Sewing Information). To assemble front (A) sew side panels to center panel, right sides together. Clip and trim the curves and press. Sew neck facings (B) together to form a rectangle. Press seams open. Turn under the outer edge of this facing ½", press and topstitch.

3 Sew sleeves (C) to side panels, right sides together. Match the upper edge of the sleeves to the upper edge of the side panels. Sew sleeves to the back panel (D), right sides together. Match upper edges as you did to the side panels. Place the neck facing, right side to right side, over the neck opening. Pin and sew. Clip and trim. Press the neck facing to the inside and tack or topstitch to secure.

*Lappa (LAH-pah)

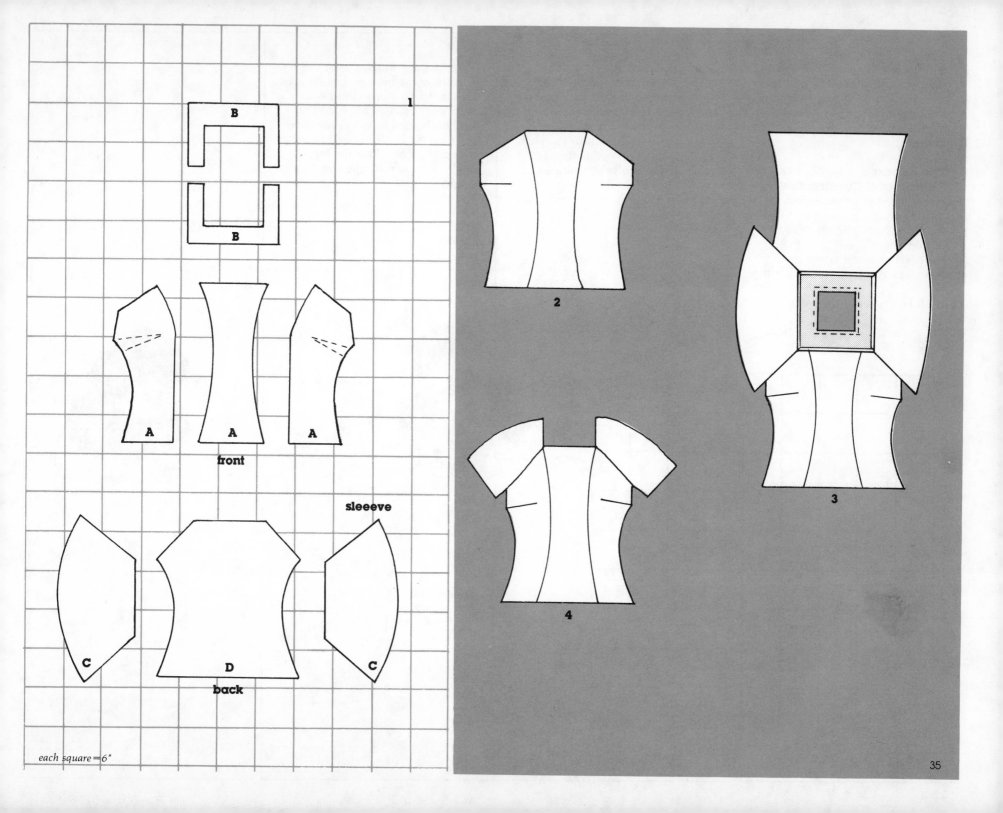

1

B
B

A A A
front

sleeeve

C D C
back

each square = 6"

2

3

4

35

4 Turn blouse, pin back to front, right sides together. Pin and sew side seams from blouse hem, along side, through underarm to sleeve hem. Hem bottom of blouse and sleeves.

The Lappa
Cutting and Construction:

Finish the ends of your cloth by turning under, pressing and top-stitching. Now you are ready to put on your Lappa. Stand with your feet shoulder-width apart; this gives you room to walk when you are dressed. Hold the lappa cloth behind you, right side out.

Start by placing the right upper corner of the cloth on the front of your left hip and hold that firmly in place. *a* The cloth goes from that hip, across your stomach, around to your back, around your left hip and across your stomach again. *b* Then roll the multiple-layered top edge of the lappa over on itself. Yes, with a firm roll, you can make your lappa stay quite securely.

West Africans usually wear the lappa over the blouse. The African finds matched lappa cloths sold in the market place. The second lap-pa cloth is used to wrap a headtie (see Chapter 2, Head-ties), to wrap around the torso over the lappa and blouse, or to drape over the shoulder.

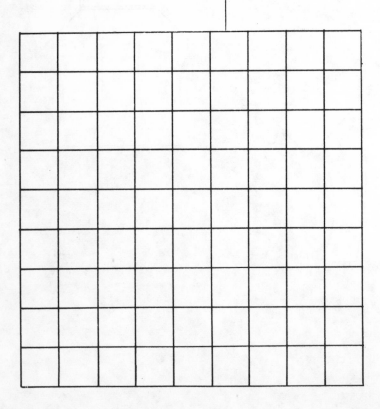

a

b

SIERRA LEONE SKIRT AND BUBA* TOP

Clothing styles of early traders and colonists still influence the current fashion of many West African nations. The resettled countries of Liberia and Sierra Leone display this factor strongly in their clothing design. This top with fitted bodice and skirt with flounce show basic elements of early colonial style retained in Sierra Leone fashion today.

Fabric Needed:
To find the amount of fabric needed for the Sierra Leone Skirt, measure from your waist to the floor, subtract approximately 15" (for the flounce) and multiply by two. Then add 45" for the flounce fabric.

Total fabric suggested for average height (5'6"):
Sierra Leone Skirt, 3 yards of 45" fabric; Buba Top, 1 yard of 45" fabric and ⅔ yard of lining, thread, 9" zipper for the top and 7" zipper for the skirt.

Buba Top
Cutting and Construction:
Before you mark your Buba Top with fabric marker on the material, check your bust and waist measurements (see appendix, Measurement Chart). To each, add a minimum of 2" of total seam allowance plus 1" of ease. Make adjustments to the pattern according to your personal measurements.

1 Mark and cut fabric. Line the top by cutting the front and back portions only from ⅔ yard of the same fabric or a lining fabric.

2 Sew bust darts as indicated (see General Sewing Information). Baste large box pleat in place on both front and back flair by folding the inside markings over to meet the outside markings. Sew the front bodice (A) to the back (B) with right sides together at the shoulder and the sides. Sew the flairs (C) together right side to right side, along the side edges.

3 Then attach the flair to the upper portion, right sides together. Sew a 9" zipper into the left side seam following the instructions on the package. This zipper will extend 4½" down into the flair.

Pin lining to Buba Top, wrong sides together. Turn under neck edge of the lining ½" and press. Topstitch ⅛" from the edge around neck and sleeve openings. Hand sew the waist edge of the lining to the main portions of the Buba. Tack at zipper and hem.

Sierra Leone Skirt
Cutting and Construction:
1 Measure your waist, hips and total skirt length. Now mark the flounce circle 45" in diameter with fabric marker on your cloth in the following way. To determine the inside circle of the flounce, use your hip measurement plus 5 or 6

*buba (BOO-bah)

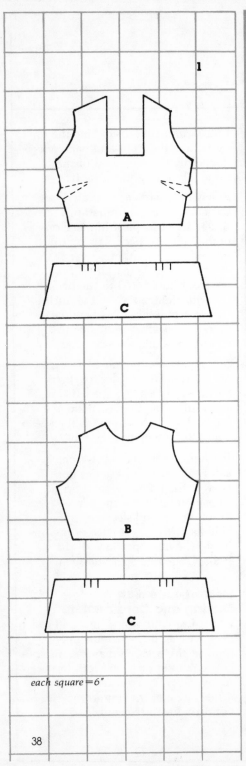

each square = 6"

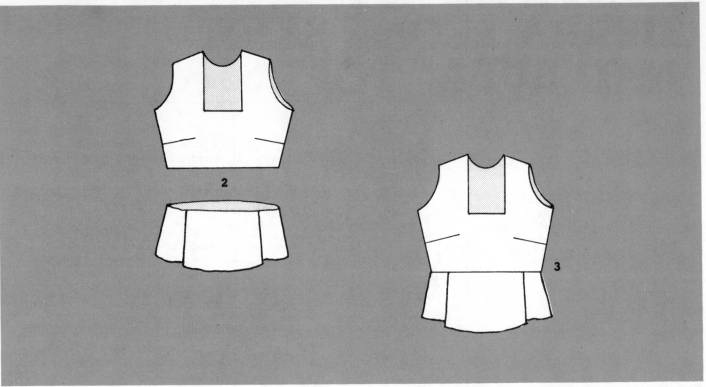

inches as the circumference. This is the measurement for the bottom edge of your upper skirt and also the circumference of the flounce inner circle. Calculate the radius of the inner flounce circle by the following simple formula:

½(circumference divided by 3.14) = the radius

example:

$3.14 \overline{)47.1''} = 15''$ (diameter)

½(15") = 7.5" (radius)

For easy marking, cut a 45" square of your fabric for the flounce. Locate the exact center and mark it. Now tie a string around your fabric marker and cut the string at 22½". Pin the end of the string to the center point and mark the

outer circle of your flounce (45" in diameter). Now cut the string to the radius number you calculated for your personal measurements. Pin it again to the center point and mark the inner circle. Cut along these lines. This is your skirt flounce.

To find the length of the upper part of your skirt, subtract the depth of the flounce from your original overall skirt length. Allow 1" for the seam where the flounce attaches. Using your hip measurement (allow 2" for ease) and your waist measurement, mark and cut the front (B), the two back panels (C), and your waistband (D).

2 Sew the darts as marked. Sew the two back panels together, right side to right side inserting the 7" zipper following instructions on the package. Then place the front on the back, right sides together, and sew the side seams.

3 Fold the waistband lengthwise in half with right sides together and sew each end straight across. Clip the corners, trim, turn right side out and press. Pin the waistband on the skirt waist, right sides together, and sew. Press under ½" along the free edge of the waistband and hand stitch it to the inside of the skirt waist. Attach a hook and eye to fasten. Attach the flounce to the bottom of the assembled skirt, right sides together. Hem.

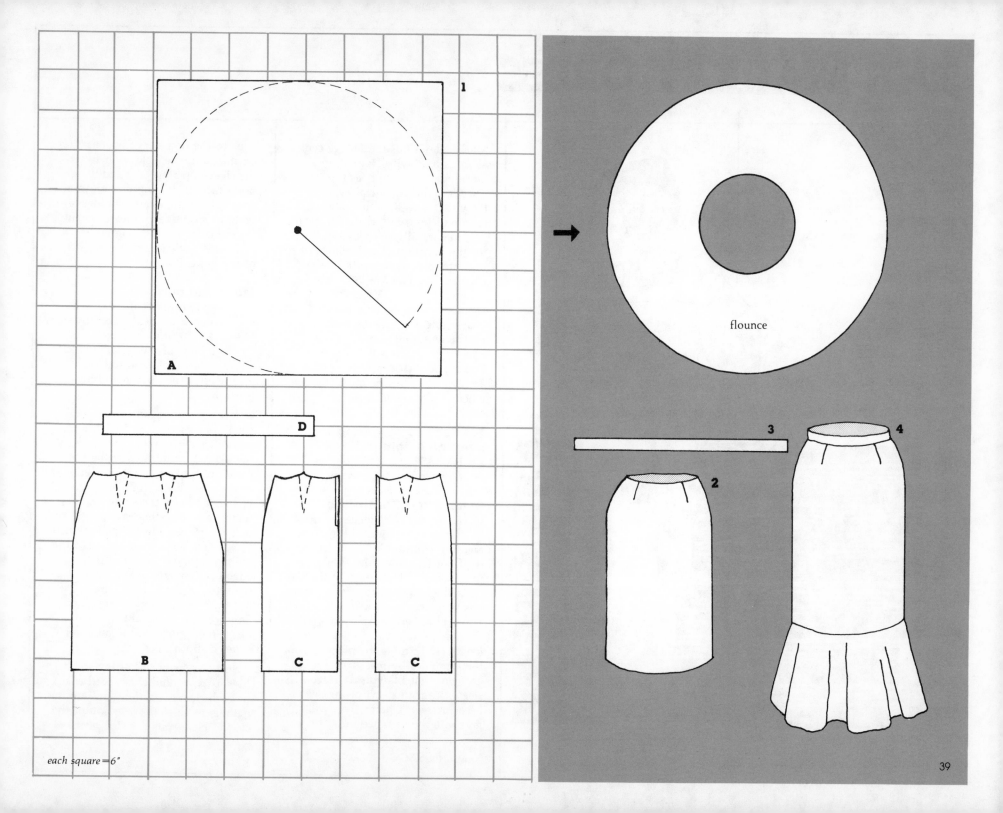

each square=6"

A

D

B

C

C

1

flounce

3

2

4

39

THE MARKET DRESS

Market day finds the village center alive with activity from early morning. Everyone goes to market since it is the big social event of the week as well as the major source of food and clothing. Each person carefully selects an outfit for the occasion. The fashions of one African country often influence others. The Market Dress is adapted by West Africans from the Ugandan dress called a busuti.* It is a simple and elegant variation on the wrapping theme.

Fabric Needed:
The Market Dress is most effective when you make it of a lightweight cloth, such as silk or rayon.

Total fabric suggested for average height (5'6"): 7⅓ yards of 45" fabric, 2 buttons, 1' of 36" pellon, 1 large snap.

Cutting and Construction:
1 To determine the length you need for the main portion of the dress, measure from under your arm to the floor (see appendix, Measurement Chart). The width of the fabric is the length of the dress, so unless you have extremely wide cloth you will have to seam two widths of material together to get your length. Determine the placement of the armholes by measuring, on a garment that fits you well, from sleeve seam to sleeve seam (see Measurement Chart). This will give you the distance from the edge to the first sleeve opening, (c) on diagram, the distance between the sleeve openings (b) and the distance (a) which continues on to accommodate the wrap. The sleeve seam to sleeve seam measurement (as indicated on the diagram) is also used to determine the length of the yoke.

Mark and cut:
A—one main piece, B—the sash, C—two each of the 3 yoke pieces, D—two each of the sleeves, E— two each of the square gussets. Turn under, press and topstitch each end of the long main body portion.

2 Sew the wrong side of one of each yoke piece to its matching piece of pellon by basting close to the edge. Pin the ends of the yoke front and yoke tab onto the ends of the yoke back, right sides together, and sew the shoulder seams. Sew together the second set of yoke pieces. Pin the pellon-lined yoke, right sides together, onto the plain yoke and sew all of the inner edge plus the end of the front overlap (where you will make the button holes). Clip corners, trim and press so that right sides are out. Press under ½" on all outer edges of both sides of the yoke.

3 Sew two rows of basting stitches ¼" apart around the curved edge of each sleeve. Partially pull up the gathers to form the puff cap of the sleeve. Next, pin one side of the

*busuti (boo-SOO-tee)

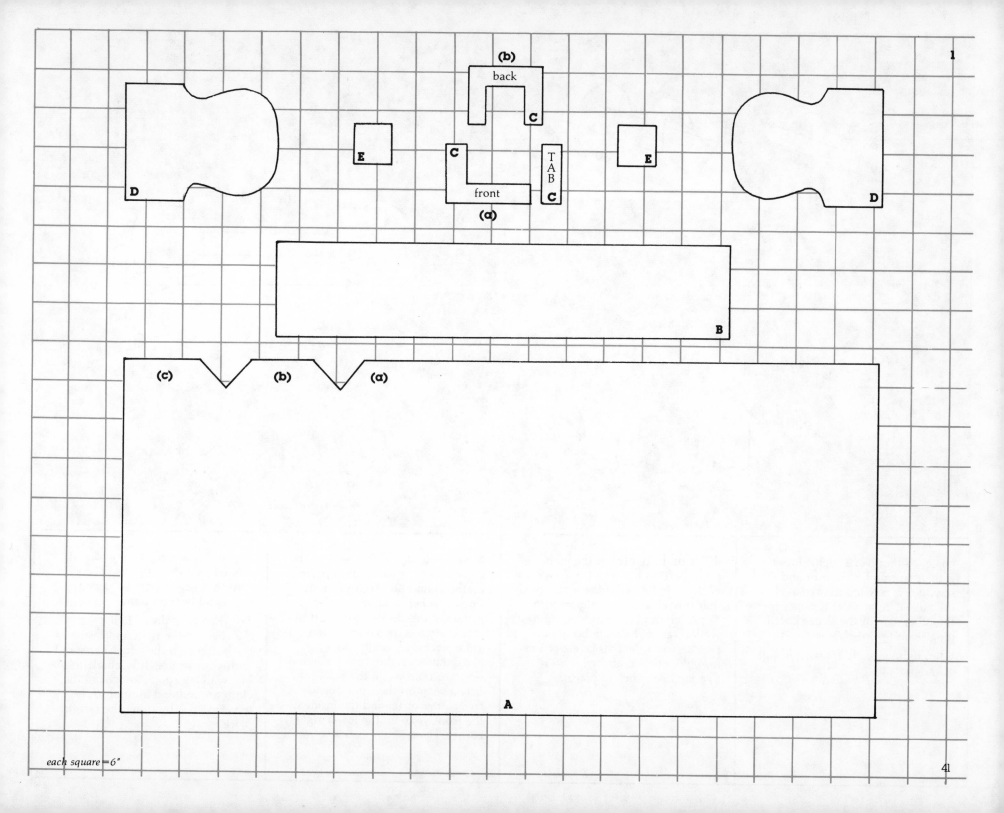

(b)

back

C

(a)

C

front

TAB

C

E

E

D

D

B

(c)

(b)

(a)

A

each square = 6"

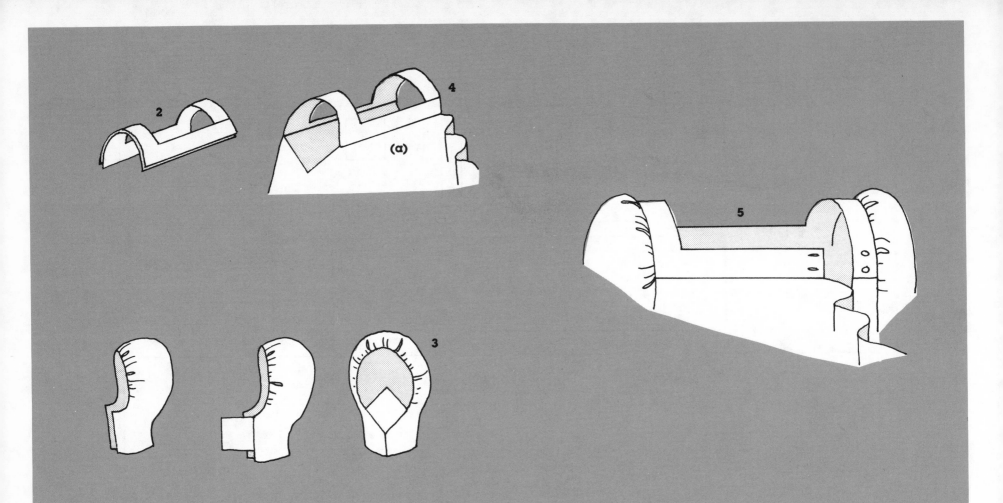

gusset to the sleeve, right sides together, just under the arm and sew. Now, sew the next edge of the gusset, right sides together to the other side of the sleeve continuing seam to finish sleeve.

You are now ready to assemble all of the parts.

4 For back, pin (b) of the main body portion between the 2 layers of the (b) portion of the yoke so that it overlaps approximately ½". Topstitch in place. For front, pin section (a) of the main body portion between the two layers of the (a) yoke portion also with a ½" overlap. Topstitch in place.

5 Assemble sleeves by pinning the gussets to each triangular opening on the main body section, right sides together, and sew. Finish gathering the sleeves to fit and pin them between the layers of the yoke piece and stitch. Make two buttonholes on the front yoke and sew two buttons on the yoke tab. Sew a snap on the front outside free corner of (c) and the inside of the front yoke on the lower right corner. Hem.

To finish the sash, turn under all raw edges ¼" and press. Then turn that edge under ¼" again. Press and hem by hand.

To wrap your dress, first secure the snap on the right and fasten the buttons on the left. Now stand with your legs slightly apart, to allow walking room, and wrap the cloth around and around to the left. Fasten it by tying the sash in place.

CHAPTER 4/
MEN'S GARMENTS

RIGA* AND ROUND HAT

*Riga (REE-gah)

Influenced by Moslem culture over centuries, the West African man often wears a long flowing robe (called riga by the Hausa tribe of Nigeria). Often seen in striking white or brilliant colors, the robe drapes and flows regally. This version is completely open on the sides, making it both cool and versatile. Men often gather the open sleeves onto their shoulder.

Fabric suggested:

African men's robes vary from heavy handspun and handwoven strip cloth to medium or light-weight commercial cotton.

Fabric required for average height (5'11"):
Riga, 3⅔ yards of 60" wide fabric or 6⅔ of 45" fabric, thread; Round Hat, ⅓ yard of 36" fabric, thread.

Riga
Cutting and Construction:

1 Measure from the shoulder ridge (see appendix, Measurement Chart) to desired length allowing an additional 2" for hem. Multiply by two for the length of the Riga (A). Fabric which is 60" wide is ideal for this outfit, but if necessary you can use 45" fabric and seam an 8" strip on each side edge. Mark fabric for shoulder line. Place the chosen neck template on the body of the Riga at the shoulder line (see appendix, Neck Opening Templates) and mark. Template V is shown in the illustration. Also mark the neck opening on a separate cloth for the neck facing (B). Traditionally a small slope of embroidered cloth (C) called linzami† is inserted on the front right side of the neck opening (optional) and a large embroidered pocket (D) is sewn off to the left, just below the neck opening. Mark and cut all pieces.

†linzami (lin-zah-mee)

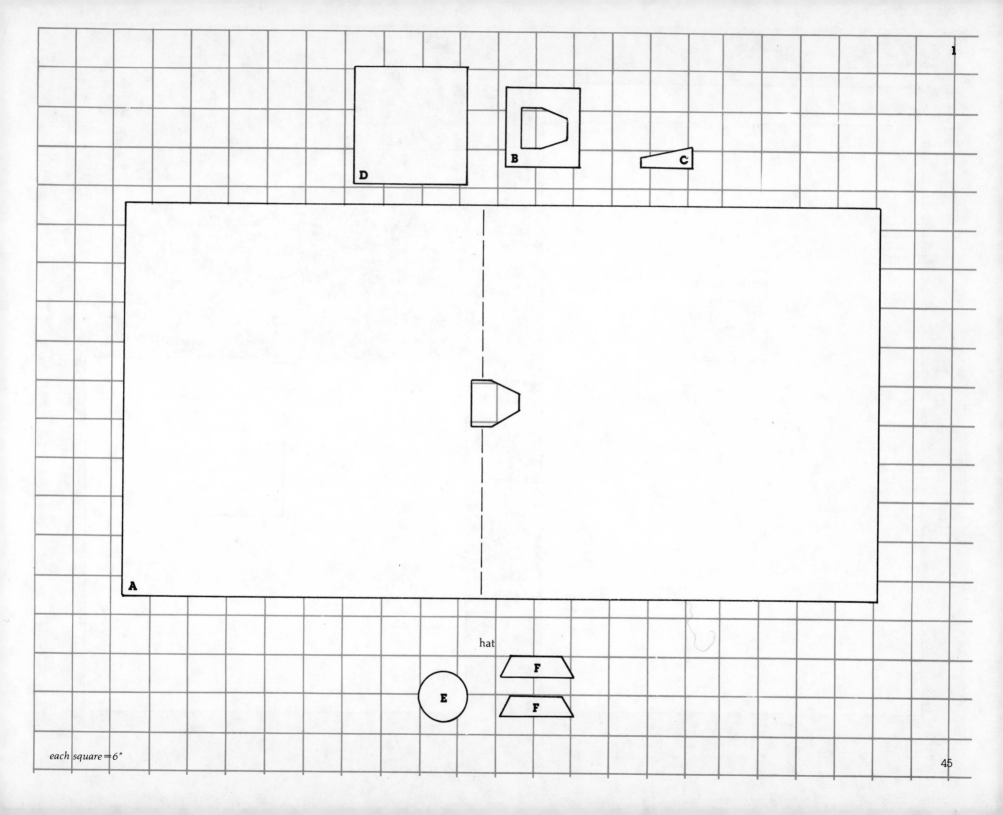

1

D

B

C

A

hat

F

E

F

each square = 6"

45

hat

2

4

5

3

46

2 Turn under ½" on all outer edges of the neck facing. Press and topstitch. Place the neck facing on the body of the outfit, right sides together. Be sure to match the neck openings. Pin and sew around the opening. Clip and trim the curves. Turn the facing to the inside and press. Topstitch or tack in place. If you are using 45" wide fabric, cut and sew 8" wide strips onto the side edges. Be sure to place the selvages on the outside edges so that no finishing will be necessary on those. Hem the Riga.

3 If desired, you can sew the side seams, right sides together, leaving 8" open at the top for each armhole. Attach the neck insert if desired. The Riga is impressive with a large hand-embroidered pocket.

Round Hat
Cutting and Construction:
The men of West Africa often wear hats. The simple hat shown is based on a circle. It is usually constructed from a heavy, self-supporting fabric. For an adult man, cut the top circle (E), 7" in diameter.

3 For a good fit, the band is constructed in two sections (F). The upper edge of each section is 10" in length. To determine the size of the hat, measure around your head at the level where the hat will be worn. Divide this figure in half and add 1" for the seam allowance. This is the length of the lower edge of each band piece. The normal finished height is 3". Allow for seam and hem.

4 Sew the two band sections, right sides together, at one end. This forms a V shaped piece. Now sew the upper, smaller edge of this band to the circle, right sides together. Sew the remaining end seam on the band, right sides together. Clip and trim the circular seam. Hem.

AGBADA* AND OVAL HAT

The Agbada worn by Yoruba men is a unique variation of the basic rectangular robes of West Africa. While the main section is still a rectangle, the wing-like sleeves are attached perpendicularly to the main body section. These robes are usually constructed from hand-woven strips, 3" to 6" wide, creating a striped effect which is vertical on the body and horizontal on the sleeves. The pouch pocket, often found on men's garments, is both functional and decorative. The pocket and neckline are finished with elaborate embroidery.

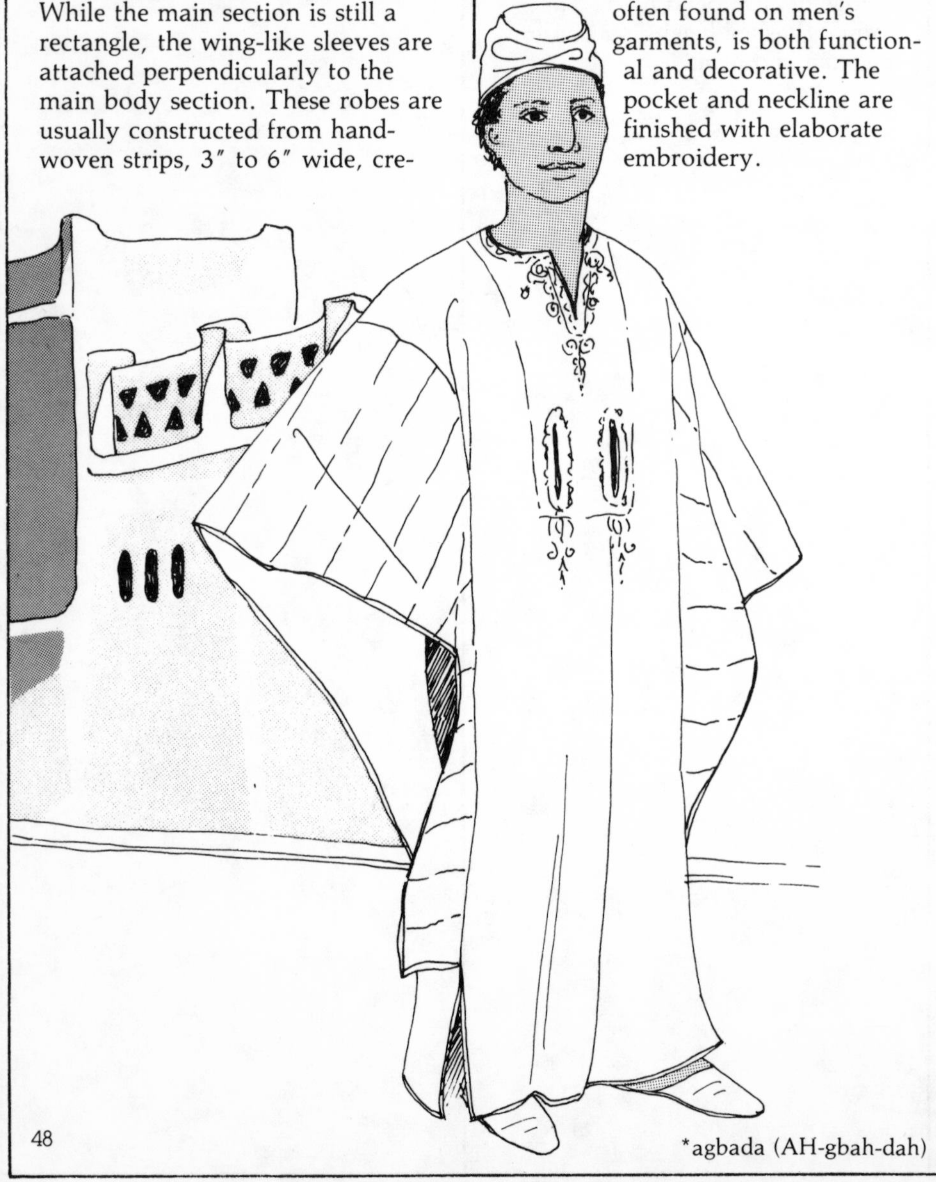

Agbada
Cutting and Construction:

1 To find the length of the main body section (A), measure from your shoulder ridge (see appendix, Measurement Chart) to desired length, allowing for hem, and multiply by two. This gives you the length of the main section. Mark the desired neck opening from the templates (see appendix, Neck Opening Templates) onto the main section at the shoulder line and onto a separate piece for the neck facing (B). Template I is shown in the illustration. Mark the 4 sleeve sections (C) (place the arrows with the grain of the fabric). Mark the pouch pocket backing (D). Cut all pieces.

2 Turn under, press and topstitch the outer edge of the neck facing ½". Place the neck facing on the main section, right sides together. Match up shoulder line marks and neck openings. Sew around the neck opening. Clip and trim the curves. Turn the facing to the inside, press and tack in place or topstitch.

3 Sew the top seams of each sleeve, right sides together and press open. Sew each sleeve to the main section, right sides together, lining up the shoulder line and the seam of the sleeve.

4 To finish the garment, sew the sleeve bottoms, right sides together, and sew 3" of the side seams below the sleeves. The slits on the sides allow for ease in walking. To finish, turn edge under ½", press and topstitch. Finish the sleeve outer edges in the same manner. Place the pocket backing behind the area indicated on the main section, wrong sides together. Topstitch in place. In Africa the pouch pocket openings are finished with an embroidered edge. You can also use seam binding.

Oval Hat
Cutting and Construction:

This hat, especially popular with the Yoruba, is found in other areas as well. It consists of an oval top (E) with a deep band (F). Made from a heavy fabric, it is always worn crushed, with the oval tilted forward.

For an adult man, cut the oval 7" x 6". The upper edge of the band section measures 19" long. To determine the size of the hat, measure around your head at the level where the hat will be worn. Add 1" for seam allowance. The normal finished height is 7". Allow for seam and hem.

5 Sew the shorter edge of the band to the oval, right sides together. Clip and trim the oval seam. Sew the ends of the band section, right sides together. Hem.

6 Wear the hat with the seam at the back and crush, tilting the oval forward.

*agbada (AH-gbah-dah)

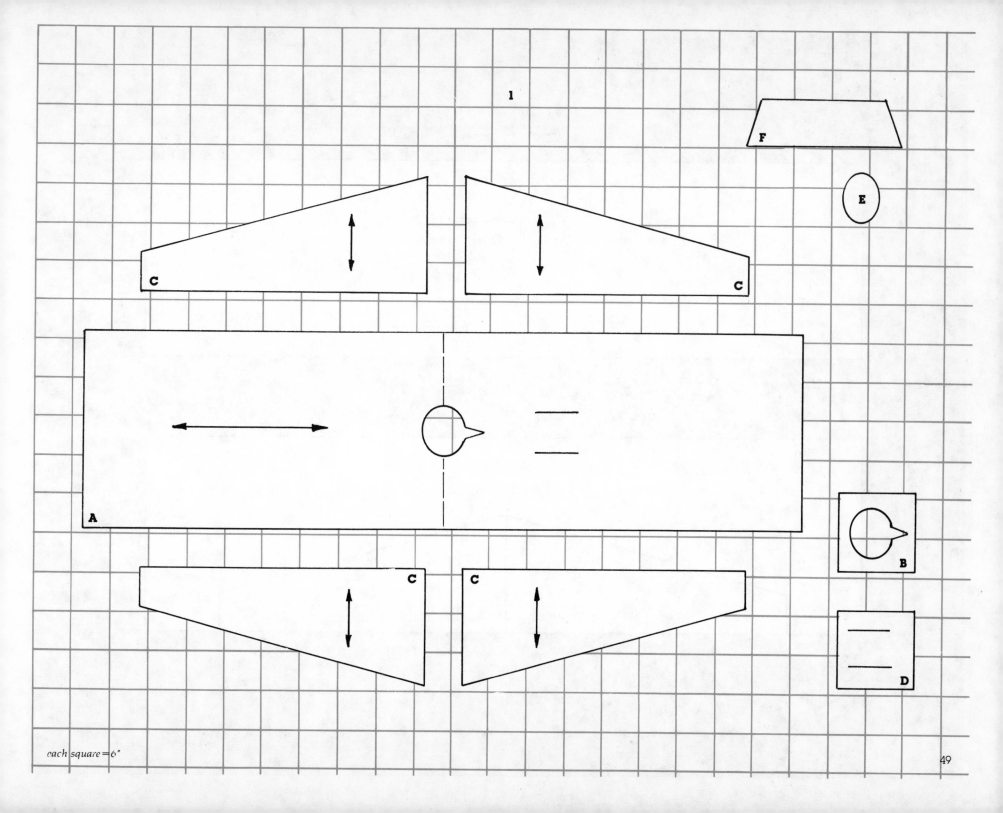

1

F

E

C   C

A   B

C   C   D

each square=6"

49

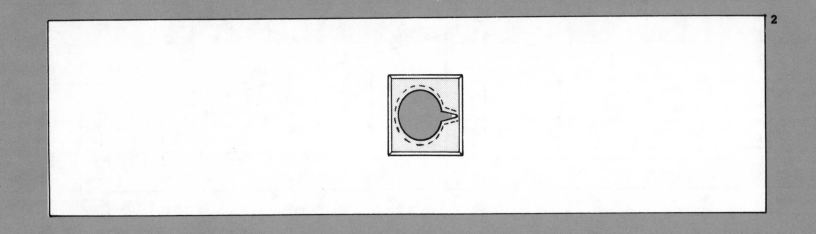

2

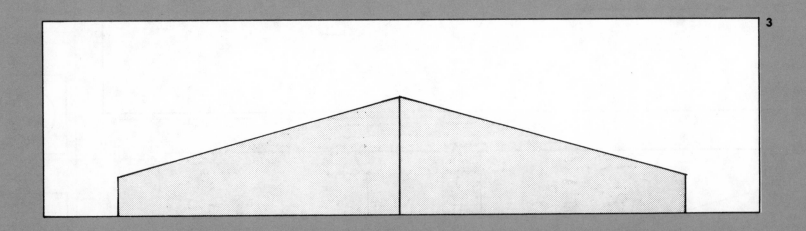

3

50

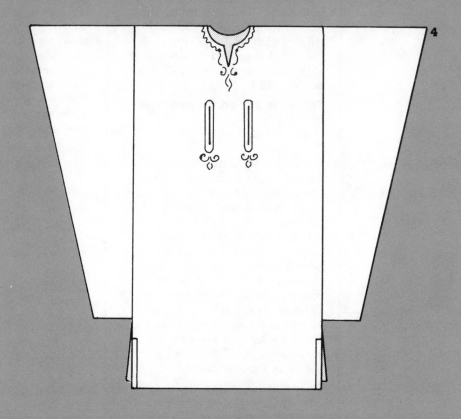

TUNIC

Men's tops in West Africa are based on a rectangle. This simple vest is traditionally worn by the men of the Bambara* [Bamana] tribe of Mali for hunting trips. It is decorated in geometric patterns with a mud dye process called bokolanfini.†

Fabric required for average build: 2⅓ yards of 36″ wide cloth, thread.

Cutting and Construction:

1 Measure from the shoulder ridge (see appendix, Measurement Chart) to the desired tunic length. Add 2″ for hem and multiply by two to get the length of the body of the tunic (A). Mark that main portion on the fabric along with 2 side strips (B), 12″ x 3″. Mark the neck opening (see appendix, Neck Opening Templates) on the main section at the shoulder line and also on a separate piece for the neck facing (C). Template I is shown in the illustration.

2 Turn under ½″ on the outer edge of the neck facing. Press and topstitch. Place the neck facing on the main section right sides together, lining up the neck openings. Pin and sew. Clip and trim the curves. Turn to the inside and press. Tack or topstitch in place.

3 Turn under ½″ of the upper edge of the side panels, press, and sew. Then, sew the side panels to the lower edges of the front of the tunic, right sides together, lining up the hems. Now sew those same side panels to the back portion of the tunic, right sides together, lining up the hems. Turn under ½″ at the arm openings, press and topstitch. Hem.

This basic tunic works well on men, women or children.

*Bambara (BAHM-bah-rah)

†bokolanfini (boh-kuh-lahn-fee-nee)

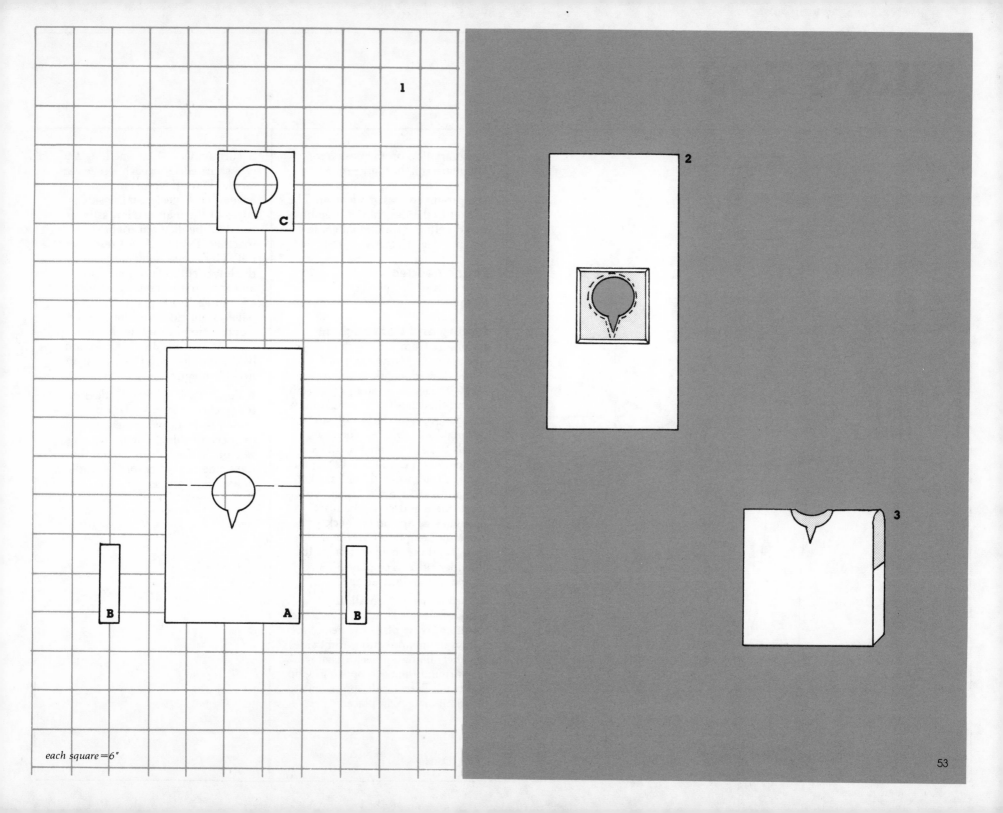

1

C

A

B   B

each square=6"

2

3

53

MEN'S TOP

This variation on the basic rectangular tunic has large open sleeves. The offset, slanted pocket is a prominent design element. The pocket in the illustration is embroidered with the traditional endless knot or dagi* (Hausa).

Fabric needed:
1⅔ yards of 45" wide fabric, thread.

Cutting and Construction:
1 Measure from the shoulder ridge (see appendix, Measurement Chart) to the desired length of the top, add a 2" hem and multiply by two to find the length of the main body section (A). The sleeves (B) are rectangles, 21" x 27". The side panels (C) are rectangles, 12" x 6". The neck facing (D) is a 12" square and the traditional slanted pocket (E) can be cut from a 12" square. Mark these and mark the neck opening (see appendix, Neck Opening Templates) on the neck facing and the main section at the shoulder ridge. Template V is shown in the illustration.

2 Turn under ½" on all outer edges of the neck facing. Press and topstitch. Now place the neck facing on the main section, right sides together, lining up neck openings. Sew around the neck opening. Clip and trim. Turn inside, press and topstitch or tack in place.

3 Turn under ½" on one long and two short edges of each sleeve rectangle. Place the remaining raw edge of each sleeve on the side edges of the main section as indicated in the diagram, right sides together. Pin and sew. Press seam flat. The sleeves remain open on the lower edge. Turn over, press and topstitch ½" on the upper edge of each side panel. Pin this panel, right sides together, to the front section below the sleeve and sew. Attach it to the back section below the sleeve in the same manner. Hem garment.

4 Turn under ½" on all edges of the pocket and press. Topstitch pocket to front of garment below the neck opening, line up the right side of the neck opening and the right side of pocket for the traditional offset effect.

*dagi (DAH-gee)

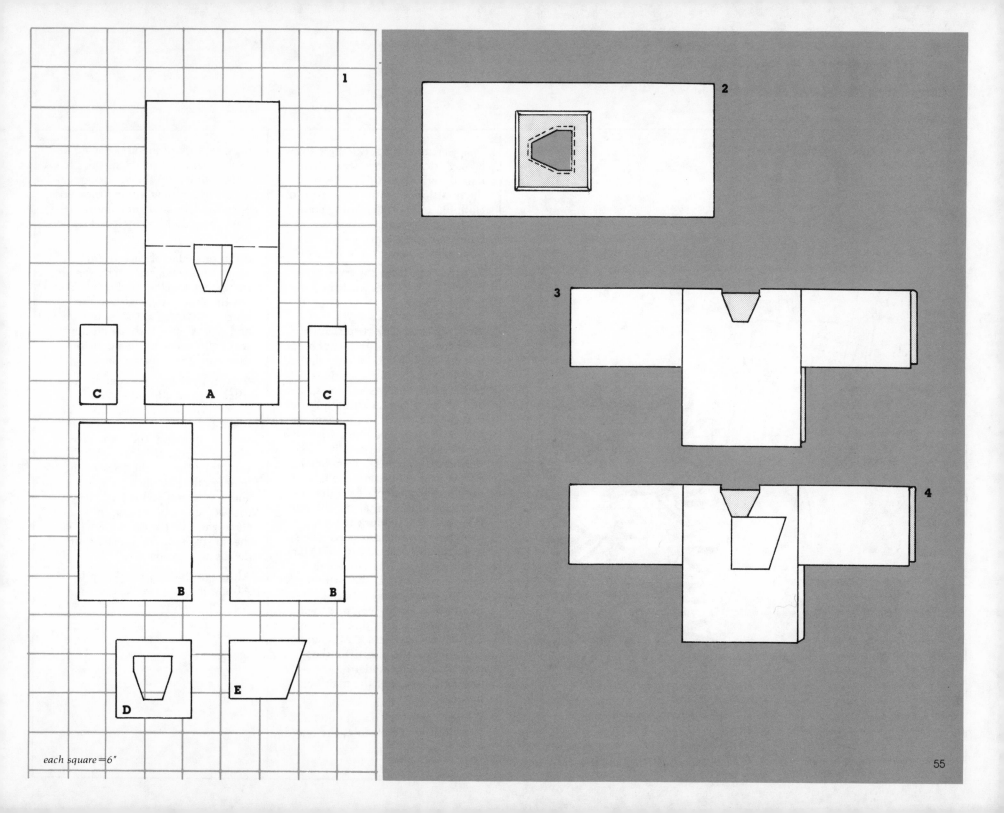

each square = 6"

55

BATIKARI*

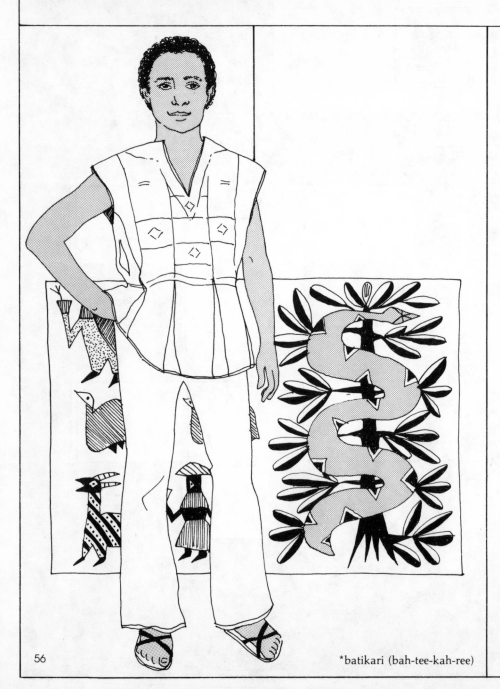

This elegant top appears in many West African communities. It is flaired and often constructed with the traditional handwoven strips of cloth (3" to 6" wide), using contrasting colors for the inserts. Some variations have sleeves, some pleats, some endless inserts.

Fabric required for average height (5'11"): 1⅓ yards of 36" fabric, thread.

Cutting and Construction:

1 Traditionally this garment comes to mid-thigh. Measure your desired length from the shoulder ridge, (see appendix, Measurement Chart) add 2" for a hem and multiply by two for the length of the main section (A) of your batikari. Choose a neck opening (see appendix, Neck Opening Templates). Template I is shown in the illustration. Place the neck opening template on the main section, lining it up at the shoulder ridge and mark. Mark the neck opening on a separate piece of cloth for the neck facing (B). Mark 2 side panels (C) 21" in length, tapering from 6" at the bottom to 3" at the top. Mark 8 triangular inserts (D), 12" in length, 3" wide at the bottom tapering to a point. Cut all pieces. Cut 4 (12") equidistant slits for the inserts on the lower front edge and 4 on the lower back edge of the main section.

2 Turn under ½" on all outer edges of the neck facing. Press and topstitch. Place the neck facing onto the main section, right sides together, lining up the neck openings. Pin and sew around the neck opening. Clip and trim. Turn inside, press and topstitch or tack in place.

3 Pin one edge of each triangular insert to one edge of each inset slit, right sides together and sew. Now pin the other insert edge to the other slit edge, right sides together and sew. Clip a V shape on the seam allowance at the point to ease pull. Press seams flat.

4 Turn over ½", press and topstitch the top edge of each side panel. Pin these panels, right sides together, to the front of the main section, lining up the hems. Sew. Now pin the side panels, right sides together, to the back of the main section, lining up the hems and sew. Press seams flat. Hem. If desired, you can include slit pockets in the side panels as shown in the illustration. For construction details see agbada.

Although this is a man's top in Africa, it is quite attractive on a woman when worn with slacks.

56

*batikari (bah-tee-kah-ree)

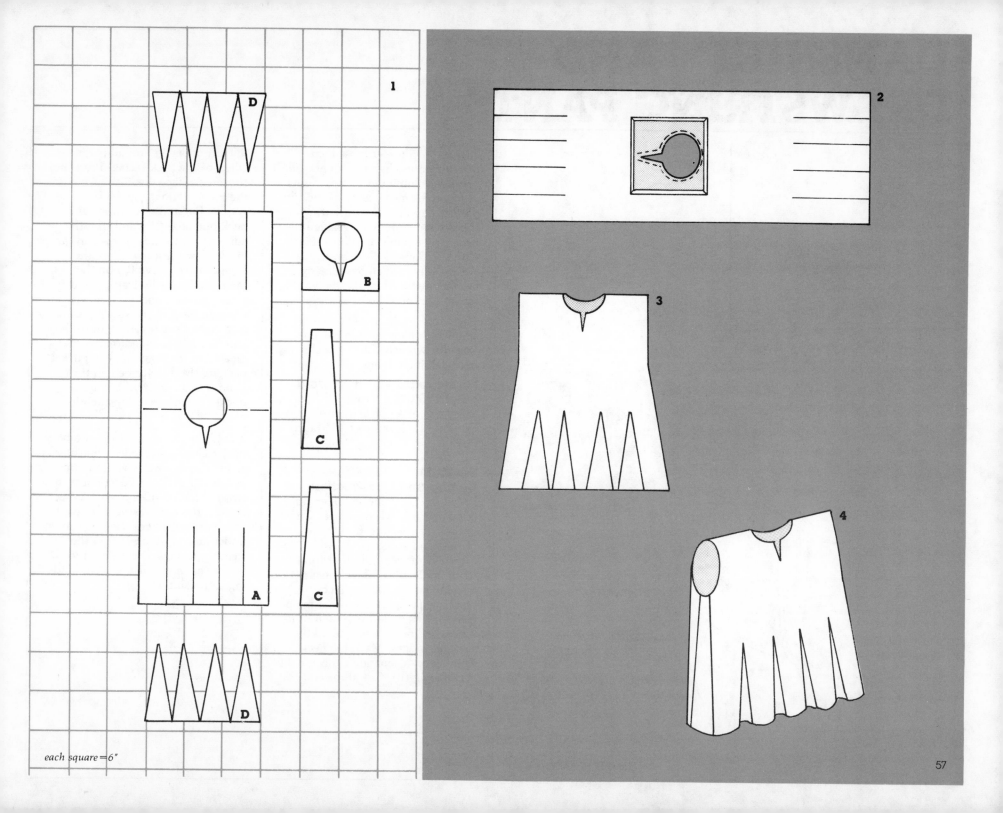

each square = 6"

57

DANSHIKI* AND DRAWSTRING PANTS

African men prefer loose comfortable pants. Early accounts tell of truly voluminous pants. (Some in museums measure 20' wide.) In present-day Africa, Drawstring Pants have more manageable fullness. These pants are illustrated with the Danshiki, the basic African shirt which has already become popular around the world for its comfortable fit.

The Drawstring pants are easily adapted to high fashion evening wear for women. Choose a slippery, feminine fabric.

Fabric required for average height (5'11"): Drawstring Pants, 3⅓ yards of 45" fabric, thread; Danshiki, 1⅔ yards of 45" fabric, thread.

Danshiki
Cutting and Construction:
1 Measure from the shoulder ridge (see appendix, Measurement Chart) to desired length to find the length of the main section (A). Add 2" for the hem. Multiply that total figure by 2. Mark the chosen neck opening (see appendix, Neck Opening Templates) on that main section. Template I is shown in illustration. Be sure to line up the shoulder ridges. Mark the neck opening on a separate cloth for the neck facing (B). Cut all pieces.

2 Turn under ½" on all outer edges of the neck facing. Press and topstitch. Place the neck facing on the main section, right sides together. Pin and sew around the neck opening. Clip and trim the curves. Turn inside, press and tack in place or topstitch. Place the edge of each sleeve (C) on the main section as indicated, right sides together, and sew. Sew two edges of each of the small gussets (D), right sides together, onto the garment at the underarms as indicated in the diagram. Pin pocket backing (E) directly behind the main section where the pouch pocket is indicated; topstitch in place.

3 Fold the Danshiki at the shoulder line, right sides together. Starting at the sleeve edge, sew along the bottom of each sleeve, connect the two remaining sides of each gusset and continue down the sides of the garment to the hem. Hem. Turn under and topstitch ½" on the sleeve openings. Embroider the pocket openings or use seam binding to finish the edges.

*danshiki (DAHN-shee-kee)

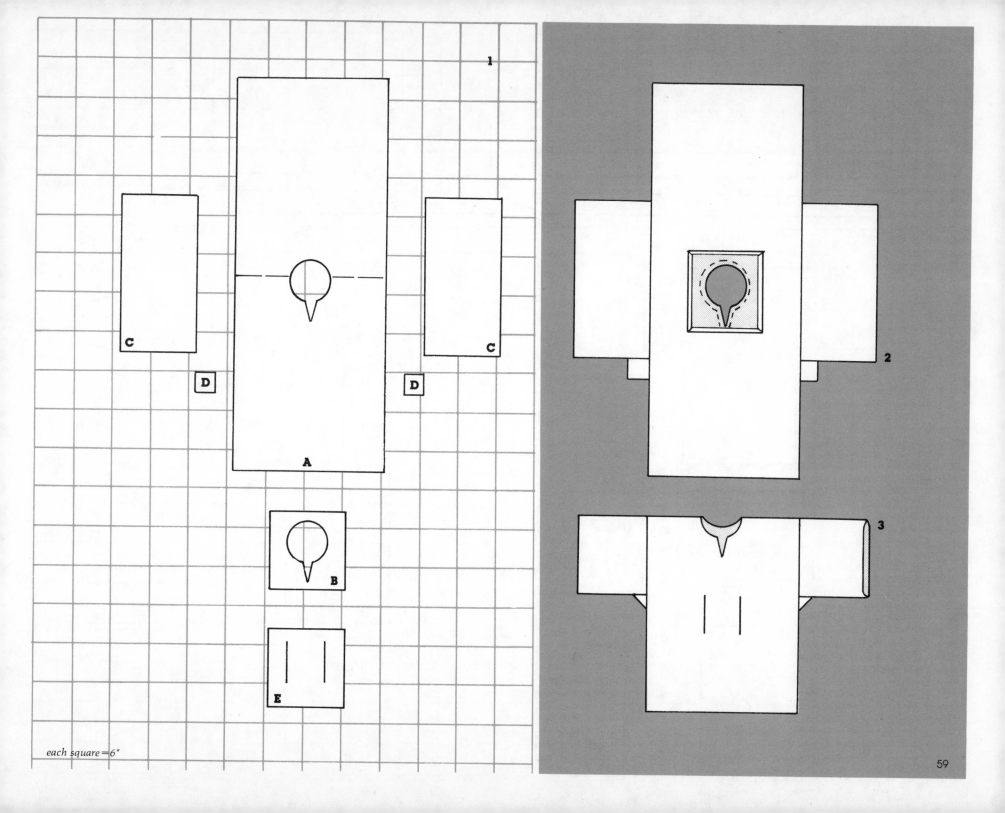

each square = 6″

1

C

D

C

D

A

B

E

2

3

59

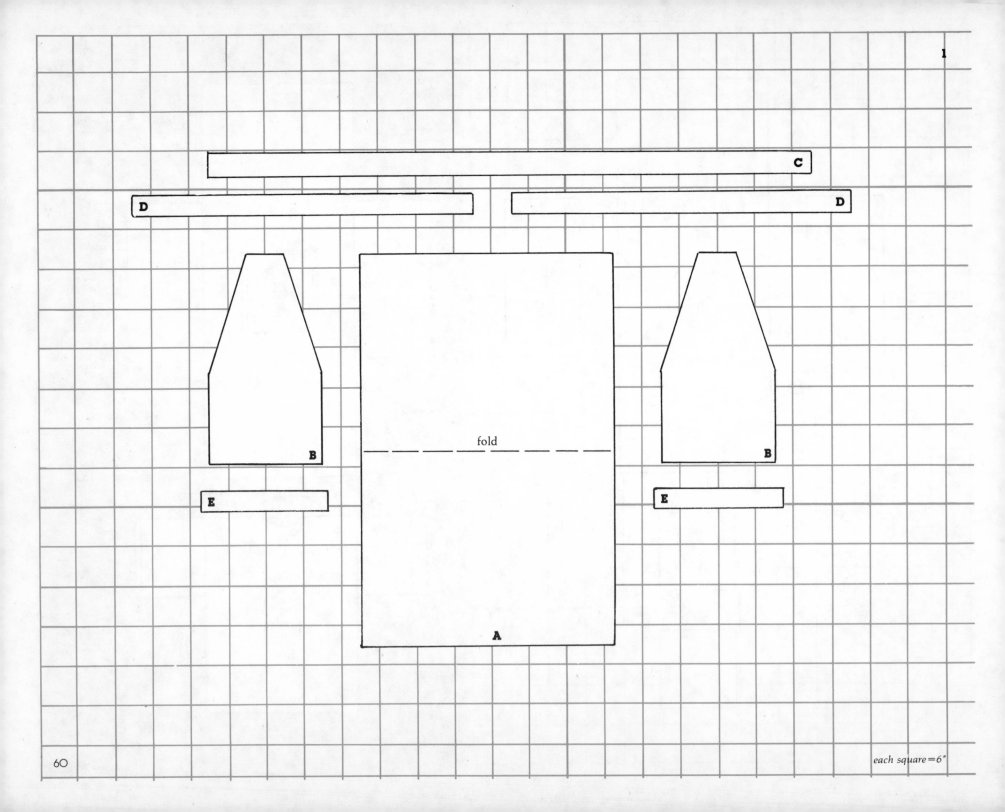

C

D   D

fold

B   B

E   E

A

each square=6"

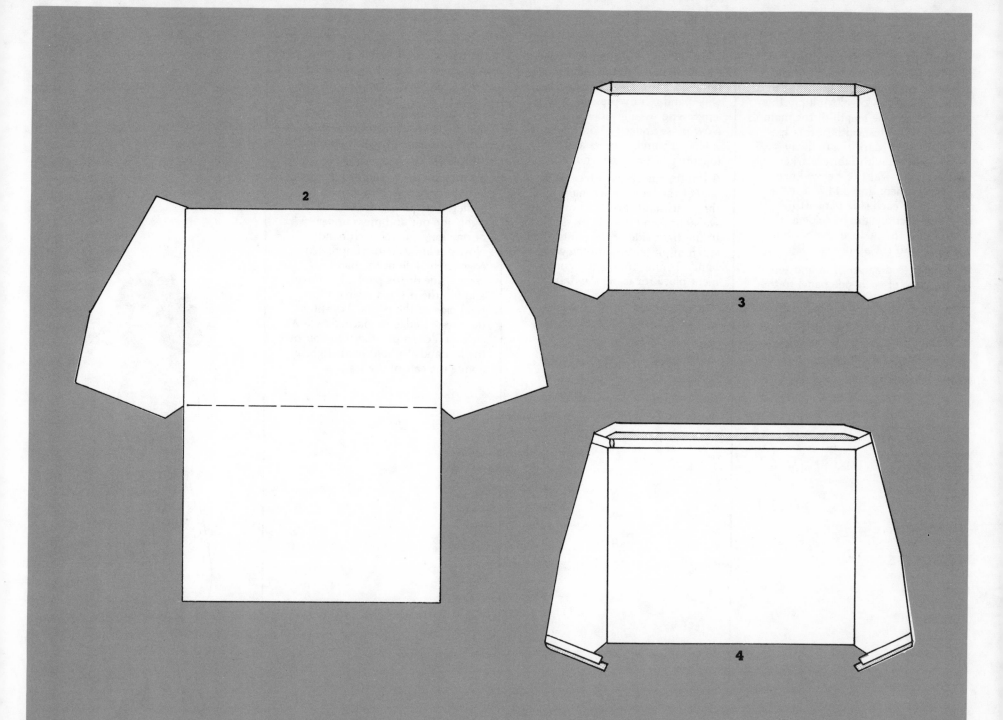

2

3

4

Pants
Cutting and Construction:

1 To determine the length of the pants, measure from the waist to just below the knee. Multiply this by two for the length of the main panel (A). The width of this section is 40". Mark the midway point (fold) with fabric marker. Take your waist-to-below-knee measurement and add 2" for the length of each side panel (B). These sections are 6" wide at the top and 16" wide at the bottom. Mark and cut all pieces.

2 Refer to diagram. Pin and sew one edge of each side panel to the main panel, right sides together, lining up the pieces at the waistline. Allow 2" of the side panel to remain unsewn below the midway mark on the main panel.

3 Now fold the main panel to the waistline and sew the other edge of each side panel to the main panel, right sides together. Prepare the waistband (C) by pressing it in half lengthwise, wrong sides together. Now press under ½" on one long side. Turn under, press and topstitch ½" on each end.

4 Pin the unpressed edge, right side of the band to wrong side of the pants, and sew. Fold over the waistband and pin the pressed edge to the right side of the pants. Topstitch in place. Be sure the waistband opening comes at a convenient place for using the drawstring.

To prepare the drawstring (D), sew the two sections together at one end. Press in half, lengthwise, right sides together. Sew closed on one end and along the long side. Turn right side out and topstitch the remaining end. Thread the drawstring through the waistband and knot the ends.

To prepare the legbands (E), press in half lengthwise, right sides together. Sew across the ends. Turn right side out and press under ½" of one long side of each band. Now pin and sew the unpressed edge, right side of the band to wrong side of the pants. Fold over and pin the pressed edge on the right side of the pants. Topstitch the pressed edge in place. Sew a 3" strip of Velcro or other fastener on the legbands to hold pants tightly above the calf of the leg.

CHAPTER 5/
FABRIC EMBELLISHMENTS

FABRIC EMBELLISHMENTS

Cloth is a prized possession in all West African cultures. Africans for centuries have given prestige to inventive techniques of fabric decoration. Textiles are both social status symbols and truly appreciated art.

The present-day cultures and textiles of Africa draw on a long and rich heritage. Accounts from early expeditions to West Africa describe elegant women, regal men, and beautiful handmade fabrics. These are evidence of elaborate cultures. Indeed, the history of black Africa dates well before 1200 B.C. when the Carthaginians began to trade on the upper Niger.[1]

By examining existing garments, we can see that outside cultures influenced textile and clothing design across West Africa. This history includes the influx of both Arabs and Europeans. Starting in the 8th century A.D.,[2] Arabs from North Africa came across the parched Sahara and established regular trade routes to obtain gold. These trade routes are still active today. One can see strong Arab influence in the dress of those peoples on the southern edge of the Sahara. The Portuguese sailed into West Africa in the mid-1400s[3] and other Europeans followed. Thus, outside influence shows up along the coastal area where early interest in slave trade and gold brought settlements of colonists.

Dyes
As elsewhere, dyes in Africa were made from natural sources. Tree bark, leaves, roots, insects, minerals in the earth, these were all used to obtain colors to enhance the cloth. The most popular of these were indigo (blue), kola nut (golden brown), and camwood (red). In the late 19th century synthetic dyes were introduced by the Europeans. Synthetic dyes are now used extensively and sometimes combined with the few natural dyes still being used. Of all the dyes used in West Africa one stands out as the most popular, indigo.

Indigo—the preferred dye
West Africans prefer indigo over all other dyes. While its origins in Africa are not certain, indigo is found in the artifacts of early cultures. In other parts of the world it can be dated back some 4,000 years. Surely it is the oldest known dye still in popular use.

In Africa the use of indigo involves mystery and ritual. Many legends tell of this "gift of blue from the heaven."[4] In each society, specific restrictions exist for its preparation and use. In most cultures the women prepare it in large pottery containers. They worship specific goddesses to insure a successful dye bath. In Northern Nigeria, however, it is the Hausa men who are the dyers. They use cement pits in the ground. In each case the opposite sex is often forbidden to enter the compound, since they believe that would ruin the dye!

Much of the mystery and ritual attached to this dye relates to its peculiar characteristics. Indigo is one of a special class of dyes. To become water-soluble the dye must be in a reduced (no oxygen) state. It becomes permanently attached to the fiber when it is again exposed to oxygen (or oxidized).

There are many different ways of preparing indigo. Africans work primarily with the pounded leaves of the indigo plant (Lonchocarpus cyanescens)[5] and wood ash. Their method is long and tedious. I have found the following method quite reliable and relatively easy. It works best on cotton, silk and linen. The following ingredients are needed (refer to the list of supply sources at the back of the book):

> water
> synthetic indigo paste
> calcium hydroxide
> zinc metal dust

Also necessary are:
- a gram scale
- a candy thermometer
- a narrow deep enamel pot (i.e. a spaghetti pot with lid)
- a large plastic tub (i.e. a 5 gallon bucket with lid)
- a small stirrer for the enamel pot
- a dowel to stir the large tub

I recommend that you use a face mask for protection while dealing with the chemicals in their powder form and rubber gloves at all times.

[1]Kate P. Kent, *West African Cloth* (Denver, Denver Museum of Natural History, 1971), p. 1.

[2]Renee Boser-Sarivaxevanis, *Textilhandwerk in West-Afrika* (Basel, Switzerland, Museum fur Volkerkunde, 1973), p. 6.

[3]*Ibid.*, p. 7.

[4]Esther Warner Dendel, *"Blue goes for Down," Brooklyn Botanic Garden's Natural Plant Dyeing, Handbook II*, 1974, pp. 23–28.

[5]Claire Polakoff, *Into Indigo* (N.Y., Anchor Books, 1980), p. 25.

Step #1 Dye Bath

A) Put 4 gallons of water in the plastic tub

B) Mix in a small disposable jar (use the face mask):
   16 grams calcium hydroxide
    6 grams zinc metal dust
   ½ cup water
Now pour this into the water in the plastic tub and stir until dissolved. Cover and let sit for 5 hours.

Step #2 Dye Stock

A) Put one quart of water in the enamel pot and place it on low heat

B) Meanwhile, mix in a small disposable jar:
   40 grams calcium hydroxide
   15 grams zinc metal dust
   ½ cup water

C) When water in enamel pot is between 90°F and 100°F stir in 8 oz. indigo paste until dissolved. Now add the calcium hydroxide/zinc solution (Step #2B) and stir without aerating for several minutes. It's very important not to put air into the dye stock! Slowly heat to 125°F. Do not allow the dye to go over 140°F as that will probably render the indigo useless.

D) Cover, remove from heat and let sit for 5 hours.

Step #3

After the 5 hour waiting period, mix the dye stock (Step #2) into the dye bath (Step #1), stir with the long dowel, cover and let sit 5 more hours.

Step #4

Test the dye bath with a small piece of cotton. The bath itself should be an amber color. Dip the cotton into the bath, wait 30 seconds and remove it. It should turn green *immediately* and then gradually it will turn blue. If it comes out blue immediately or if your bath looks blue, you made a mistake in the process.

You are now ready to dye your cloth!

Prewet the fabric in water. Now dip it into the indigo bath, hold it there for about 30 seconds and remove it. Take care not to agitate the bath if at all possible. It is best if you don't let the piece drip back into the bath as it is airing and changing color. If you want a darker color after it has turned blue, dip it again in the indigo bath. Air again and repeat if de-

sired. When you have obtained the darkness you want, rinse the cloth with clear water to remove any dye scum from the surface, then hang it up to dry. Pieces can be dyed again after they have dried.

A metallic pinkish scum on top of the dye bath is normal. In many parts of Africa they pound this into the cloth, giving it a high sheen.

You can keep your indigo bath alive for several weeks by sprinkling a teaspoon of calcium hydroxide and a dash of zinc metal dust into the bath after you are finished dyeing for the day. Stir it, cover it and be sure it sits 5 hours before you use the bath again. You should do this even on days when you don't use the bath.

Resist Dyeing

Indigo dye is most effective when used along with a resist method. Techniques of resisting the dye from the cloth or fiber to reserve the original color are referred to as resist dye methods (called "adire"* by the Yoruba). Included in this category of surface design on fabric are mechanical techniques such as tied, sewn, folded and clamped cloth. Also included are cloths with a resisting substance applied to the surface such as paste resist (starch), batik (wax) or gutta (latex). The "adire" techniques are the dominant decoration used on West African clothing. Try samples of the following techniques.

*adire (ah-DEE-reh)

Tie-resist or tie-dye:

Most African tie-dyed cloths consist of 1 or 2 patterns repeated in infinite number to make a rich design. You are simply covering desired areas with raffia (used in West Africa), cord or thread and tying tightly to prevent the dye from penetrating the fabric under the thread.

The most basic pattern is the *rosette.* (A) Take hold of the cloth as if you are pinching it. Now bind that with thread. The farther away from your pinched fingers, the larger the circular pattern you will make. It can be secured by a simple knot, but it is more certain if you wrap the thread around several times before knotting it. To create circles within circles, (B) you can bind and knot again farther away from the pinched section. To form a large design made up of many small rosettes, group them or line them up. Use large or small rosettes for accents. Incorporate objects into your tie-dye process. For example, put a bean, pebble, or marble under the cloth and instead of pinching the cloth, simply pick up the object in the cloth and bind it in place.

Accordion pleating is another simple approach. (C) It is helpful to use an iron when making pleating. Fold the cloth back and forth on itself in even or uneven folds and press. (D) Now bind it into a closed position with thread. Faint lines will follow the folds and strong resist lines are made wherever you bind the folds together.

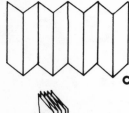

Sew-resist or tritik:

Sew-resist is accomplished with needle and thread. Here the binding penetrates the fabric. If you are working with heavy cloth or a large area, use a heavy thread such as carpet thread. The pattern is created by the puckers and folds which occur when the thread is pulled and secured. (E) *Any design* can be drawn on the cloth with fabric marker. Now sew a long running stitch along that line and pull it up, tying the ends of the thread together. It is most effective when you sew a second or multiple lines around the shape, equidistant to the first line. If you make more than one line of sewing, wait to pull any of them up until you have finished sewing all of the lines. Then pull up the one in the center first, secure it, and work your way out.

(F) You can make a very effective *spiral* pattern with long running stitches. Another way to use tritik is in combination with folding the fabric. (G) For an *edge fold* tritik, fold your cloth in half and sew a long running stitch ¼" from that fold all along the edge. Now pull up the thread firmly and secure it before dying.

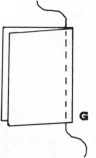

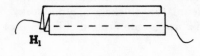

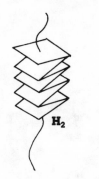

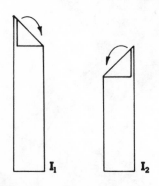

Fold-resist: Many designs are created by folding the fabric. The folded cloth is secured by tying it, sewing it or clamping it before placing it in the dye. A basic pattern I call Bompossa's Pattern (H1), I learned from a well-known Sierra Leone dyer. Fold and press a long rectangle in half lengthwise. Now fold each edge back to make a total of 4 layers of folds and press. With firm needle and heavy thread, start at one end of the folded cloth and sew a very large running stitch (1" stitches) along the center of the cloth for the entire length. (H2) Before dying, pull up the thread firmly and tie the ends. This gives an all-over checkered pattern.

Try a *triangular flag fold.* Using a long rectangle, fold it lengthwise in 3 and press. Now fold the end over diagonally until the end edge lines up on top of the side edge. (I1) Press. Fold a triangle on the other side in the other direction (I2) and press. Continue to fold in that manner until you reach the end of the fabric. (I3)Sandwich your cloth triangle between 2 small pieces of plastic or wood and clamp with a C-clamp. (I3) Now you are ready to dye for a kaleidoscope-like pattern.

Wax-resist or batik: The technique of resisting dye by applying wax to the cloth is believed to have originated many centuries ago in Indonesia. India and Egypt also show very early use of wax resist dyeing. It is unknown exactly how or when wax resist started on the African continent, but it is now a very popular fabric decoration.

The wax is heated and then applied to the cloth when it is hot enough to penetrate and does not just sit on the surface. A very satisfactory combination is 1 part beeswax to 3 parts paraffin. This gives crackle (fine lines of dye that penetrate the design), but at the same time allows the fabric to flex without cracking off the wax. Various ways of heating the wax are acceptable, a coffee can inside a pot of water on the stove, an electric frying pan, an electric tea pot. Keep in mind that there should be plenty of ventilation and that the wax should not be heated higher than needed to penetrate the cloth. Wax can self-ignite at high temperatures. Avoid accidents, *do not leave it unattended!*

The wax can be applied in several ways. The Javanese use a tjanting tool which has a metal reservoir to hold a small amount of hot wax while working. The tjanting can make fine, precise lines. A brush is also a good tool. The Africans prefer the stamp or tampon method which is comparable to the Javanese tjap. You can easily carve your own design into a piece of wood, cork, or similar material. The carved surface of the stamp is dipped in the hot wax and immediately applied to the cloth. Practice first to minimize drip marks on your final cloth. After the cloth is dyed, the wax can be removed by either boiling it (allow for shrinkage), or ironing it between layers of newsprint paper.

Paste-resist: The Yoruba women are famous for their paste resist (adire eleko)* fabrics which they wear as skirt wrappers (see Lappa, Chapter 3). Women also do much of the decorating of the fabric, although men are now involved in the stencil process. The paste, made of the cassava root, a food staple, is produced by pounding the dried root into a powder. That powder is then mixed with water for application to the fabric. Two methods of applying the paste can be used. The most traditional method is to paint on the paste with a chicken feather. More recently a tin stencil is used for less important cloths. I recommend a cake decorator or a syringe (without needle) for ease in applying the paste. You can also cut a stencil from oaktag, the paper used for common file folders. When using a stencil, hold it firmly on the cloth and brush on the paste or scrape it over the surface.

*eleko (eh-LEH-kaw)

The paste must dry thoroughly before you put the cloth in the dye. Use a dye with quick application. Indigo is used by the Yoruba. The paste comes off in water, so it can not sit in a dye bath. If the dye is applied quickly, the paste design stays in place. To remove the paste, peel it when dry or immerse it in water and scrape it off.

As I have worked with paste resist, I have devised the following recipe, based primarily on that of Lois Brooks ("Workshop: Adire Eleko," *Craft Horizons*, Aug. 1971, pp. 12–15).

Mix in blender for 1 minute:

> ¼ cup pearl tapioca
> 1 cup water

Let this sit in the refrigerator overnite, then blend again for 3 minutes and store the unused portion in the regrigerator.

Dissolve in 1 cup water:

> 2 tablespoons cassava starch
> 3 tablespoons cornstarch

Mix in blender:

> the starch mixture
> ½ cup of the tapioca mixture
> ¾ cup water

Cook in double boiler, on medium heat, stirring constantly. The mixture should become thick and translucent. Keep this warm while using. Mix only what you think you will use. If the mixture thickens as you work, stir in a small amount of water. This mixture is safe around children (not unlike the old library paste).

Block Printing

Block printing is a specialty of the Ashanti* (Asanti) tribe of Ghana, where it is called Adinkra† (Adinkera). Traditionally worn only for mourning, Adinkra cloth is now quite popular. Used in many colors for clothes, bedspreads and curtains, it represents a certain national pride. The designs are carved into pieces (usually under 3″ in diameter) of calabash gourd and a handle made of palm leaf ribs is attached. The thick, shiny black dye from the badie tree (Briaelia Micranta) is applied to the cloth with these stamps. Each stamp of traditional design has a symbolic meaning. In 1927, the researcher, Rattray, listed over 50 distinct stamp designs.[1] Most of these meanings display the values of Ashanti society. Ntesie‡ (A) "What I hear I keep." implies wisdom, knowledge and prudence. Dwenimem§ (B), the ram's head, is a symbol of humility and strength, wisdom and learning.

A large grid is created on the cloth with an African comb dipped in the badie dye. While a whole cloth may have several patterns on it, each section of the grid is filled with the repeated patterns of one stamp. Although originally made of handwoven strips, the adkinkra cloth is now made of commercial cotton cut or torn into 6 long sections approximately 15″ wide and 11′ long. These sections are embroidered together with a rainbow of bright colors in a figure-eight stitch.

[1]R.S. Rattray, *Religion and Art in Ashanti* (London, Oxford University Press, 1927), chap. XXV.

*Ashanti (ah-SHAHN-tee)

†adinkera (ah-DING-k'rah)

‡ntesie (nn-tey-see-ay)

§dwenimen (dywih-nih-mihn)

Western dyes can not mimic the luster of the badie dye. I recommend Versatex Textile Paint as a western substitute. Carve a gourd or cork with your design. It is only necessary to carve away approximately ¼″ in depth around your design. The raised part, not carved away, will print your design. Brush on the dye and press the stamp carefully onto the cloth. If you use Versatex, be sure to set it with a steam iron after it is dry.

Embroidery

Embroidery now appears on a large number of West African clothes. While several groups have done embroidered cloth, it is that embroidery done predominantly by the Hausa men of northern Nigeria that stands out for its richness and elaborate beauty. Many Hausa men today still hand-embroider elegant robes (see Riga, Chapter 5) with silk or cotton thread. Pants, caps and sometimes shoes are also embroidered and can be seen especially in the cities.

The popularity of this tradition has traveled all along the West African coast and inland along the river Niger. Embroidery done on special treadle sewing machines abounds everywhere, but hand-embroidery is almost exclusive to Hausaland. The Hausa use primarily couching, the chain stitch, buttonhole stitches and a type of needleweaving referred to as linzami.[2] (The term linzami is also used for the embroidered triangular insert as seen in the Riga illustration.)

Hausa embroidery designs

[2]David Heathcote, "Hausa Embroidered Dress," *African Arts*, Vol. V, no. 2, (Winter 1972), p. 17.

APPENDIX

Measurement Chart

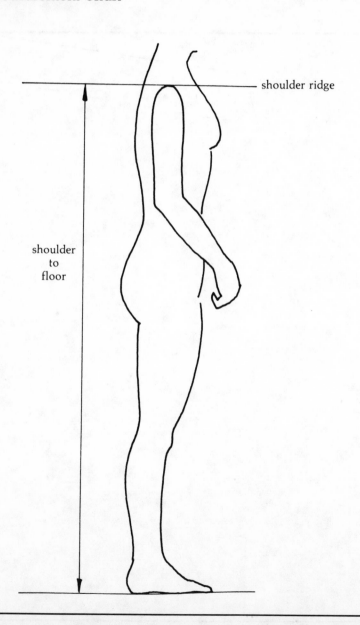

shoulder ridge

shoulder
to
floor

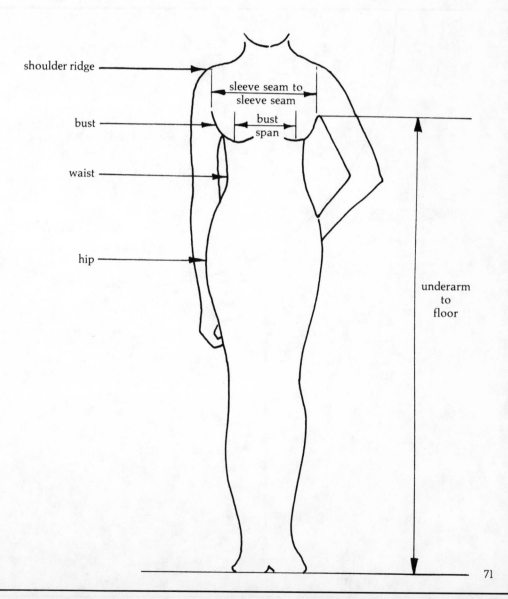

shoulder ridge

sleeve seam to
sleeve seam

bust

bust
span

waist

hip

underarm
to
floor

Neckplate Opening Template I

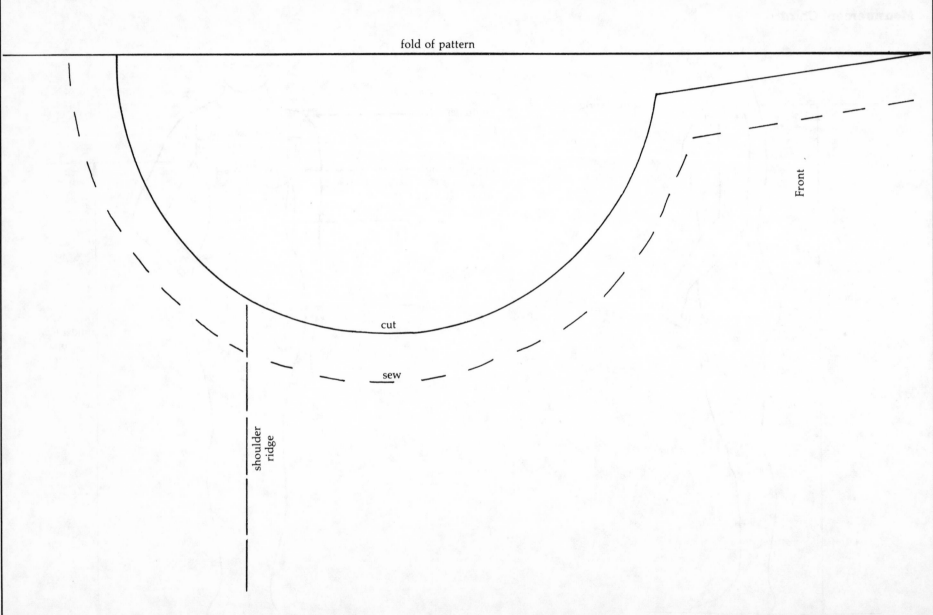

fold of pattern

cut

sew

shoulder ridge

Front

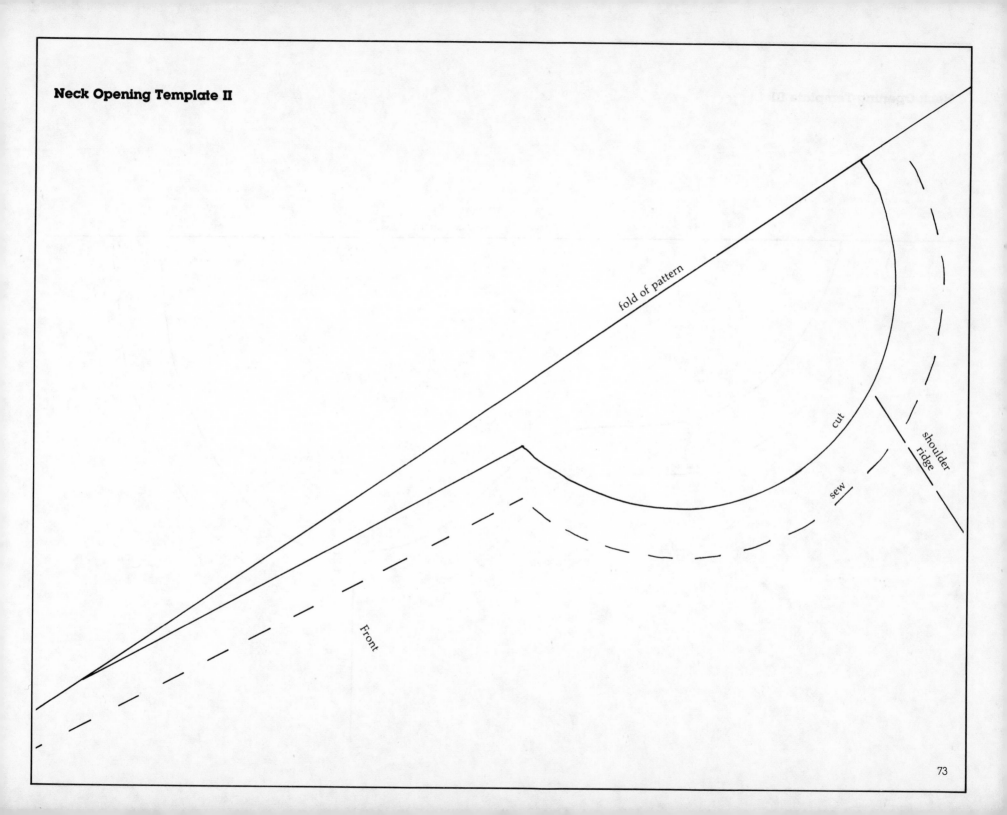

Neck Opening Template II

fold of pattern

cut

sew

shoulder ridge

Front

73

Neck Opening Template III

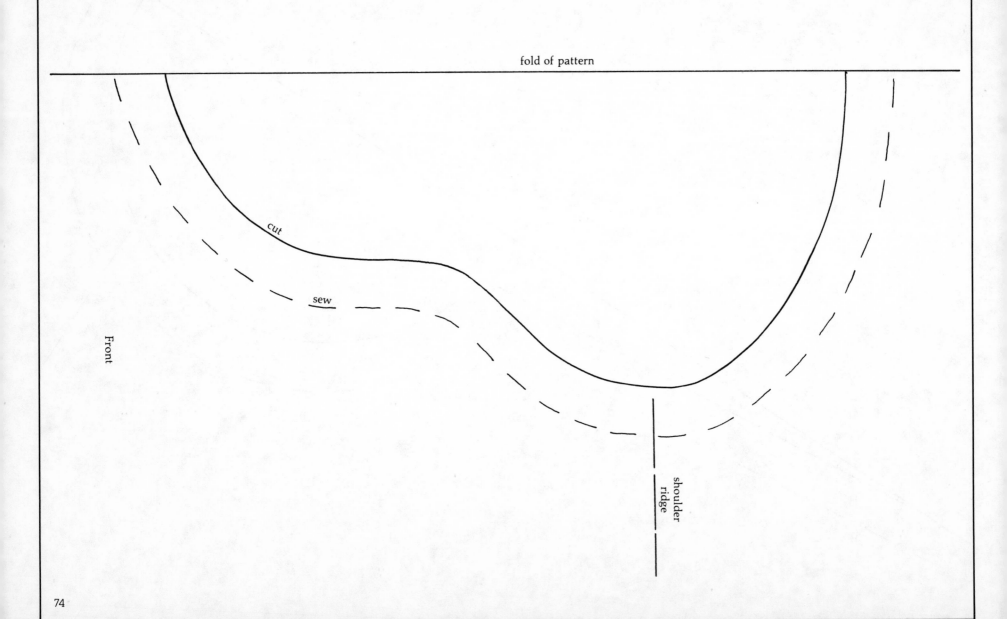

fold of pattern

cut

sew

Front

shoulder
ridge

Neck Opening Template IV

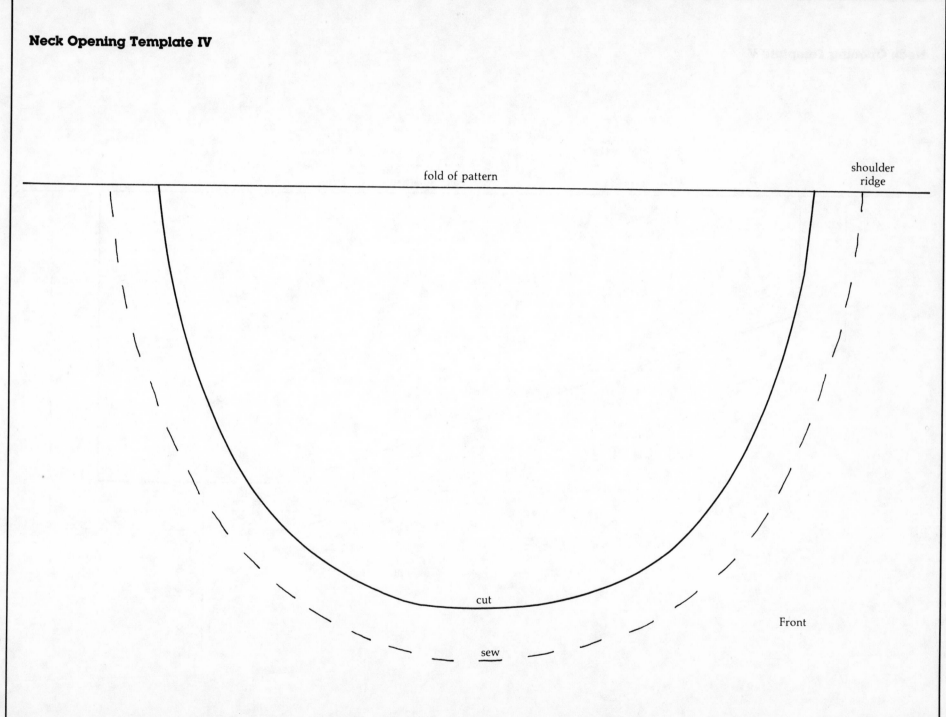

fold of pattern

shoulder ridge

cut

sew

Front

75

Neck Opening Template V

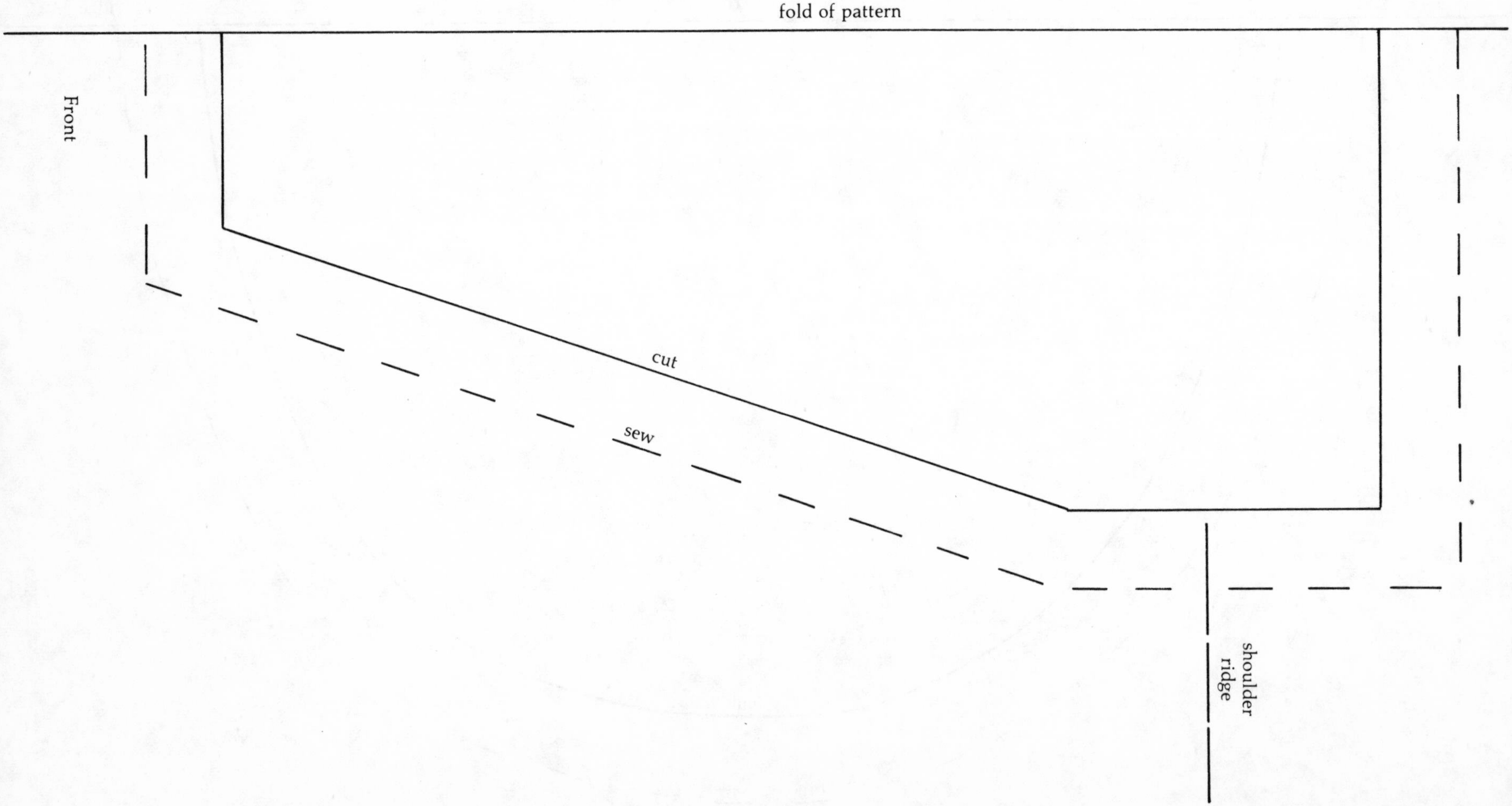

fold of pattern

Front

cut

sew

shoulder
ridge

76

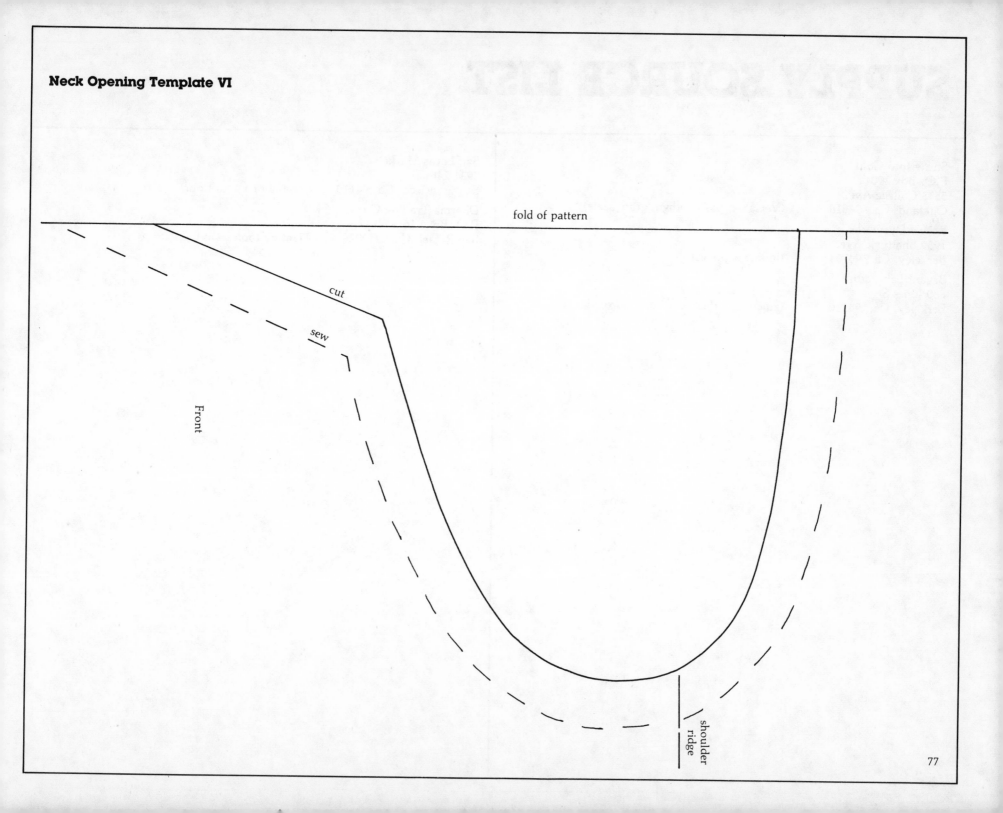

Neck Opening Template VI

fold of pattern

cut

sew

Front

shoulder
ridge

77

SUPPLY SOURCE LIST

Straw Into Gold
P.O. Box 2904
5533 College Ave.
Oakland, Ca., 94618   (Versatex, paste indigo, gram scale)

Kasuri Dyeworks
1959 Shattuck Ave.
Berkeley, Ca., 94704   (indigo supplies)

Bryant Laboratory
880 Jones St.
Berkeley, Ca., 94710   (zinc metal dust, calcium hydroxide)

San Lucas Market
2934 24th St.
San Francisco, Ca. 94110   (cassava or yucca flour)

Dharma Trading Co.
P.O. Box 916
San Rafael, Ca., 94902   (Tjanting tools, wax)

BIBLIOGRAPHY

African Garments & Textiles

Aradeon, Susan, and Nordquist, Barbara, *Traditional African Dress & Textiles*, Washington, D.C., Museum of African Art, 1975.

Boser-Sarivaxevanis, Renee, *Apercus sur la Teinture a l'Indigo en Afrique Occidentale*, Basel, Switzerland, Museum fur Volkerkunde, 1969.

_____, *Textilhandwerk in West-Afrika*, Basel, Switzerland, Museum fur Volkerkunde, 1973.

de Negri, Eve, "Yoruba Women's Costume," *Nigeria Magazine*, March, 1962, pp. 4–12.

_____, "Yoruba Men's Costume," *Nigeria Magazine*, June, 1962, pp. 4–12.

Eicher, Joanne Bubolz, *African Dress, a select and annotated bibliography of subsaharan countries*, East Lansing, Michigan State University, 1973.

Jefferson, Louise, *The Decorative Arts of Africa*, New York, Viking Press, 1973.

Kent, Kate P., *West African Cloth*, Denver, Denver Museum of Natural History, 1971.

Picton, John and Mack, John, *African Textiles*, London, British Museum Publications Ltd., 1979.

Rattray, R.S., *Religion and Art in Ashanti*, Oxford, Clarendon Press, 1927, London, Oxford University Press, 1959, 1969.

Sieber, Roy, *African Textiles and Decorative Arts*, New York, Museum of Modern Art, 1972.

Techniques

Barbour, Jane, and Simmonds, Doig, *Adire Cloth in Nigeria*, Nigeria, The Institute of African Studies, University of Ibadan, 1971.

Brooks, Lois, "Workshop: Adire Eleko," *Craft Horizons*, August, 1971, pp. 12–15.

Coats and Clark, Book #150, *100 Embroidery Stitches*, New York, 1964.

Dendel, Esther Warner, *African Fabric Crafts*, New York, Taplinger, 1974.

Heathcote, David, "Hausa Embroidered Dress," *African Arts*, Winter 1972, Vol. V., #2, pp. 12–19, 82.

Maile, Anne, *Tie and Dye as a present day craft*, New York, Taplinger, 1969.

Nea, Sara, *Tie-dye*, New York, Van Nostrand Reinhold Co., 1971.

Newman, Thelma, *Contemporary African Arts and Crafts*, New York, Crown, 1974.

Polakoff, Claire, *Into Indigo*, New York, Anchor Press, 1980.

Quarcoo, A.K., *The Language of Adinkra Patterns*, Legon, Ghana, Institute of African Studies, University of Ghana, 1972.

Wada, Yoshiko, "Dyeing with Indigo," Berkeley, Kasuri Dyeworks, 1976. (pamphlet)

The Author

A keen appreciation for the garments and fabrics of ethnic peoples led *Chris Rex* into the open markets of West African villages and the mud huts of the savanna. In 1975 she spent her sabbatical leave in five West African countries. Going from village to village, often living with the natives, she studied the many techniques of making and decorating textiles in a society where cloth is of paramount cultural importance.

After graduating from Wilson College, she earned her M.A. from Wesleyan University in Connecticut. She has also studied at Tyler School of Art, Michigan State University (Paris), Haystack, and with many prominent craftspeople around the country. Presently her personal art medium is resist-dyed fabric.

Since 1968 she has headed the art department at American River College, Placerville Campus, in the foothills of the Sierra Nevada. She also gives workshops around the country and leads textile tours abroad.

The Illustrator

Lee Fitzgerrell, a native Californian, earned her B.A. from Occidental College and her MFA at Instituto Allende in Mexico. She has been a freelance artist for fourteen years. The illustrator of several children's books and record album covers, she also does commissioned murals and paintings. Her work often reflects a dreamlike quality.